Advance Praise for
Law Firm SEO

"Jason Hennessey is the platinum standard for digital marketing and search engine optimization. In a world of so many charlatans and snake oil salesmen in the digital marketing space, he is the real deal."

—**Rich Newsome**, trial lawyer and
Founder of Trialschool.org

"Jason is a straight shooter in business and in his personal life. He is one of the most knowledgeable marketers in the industry. I go to him whenever I have questions about SEO and Google."

—**Harlan Schillinger**, Board Member of the
National Trial Lawyers Association

"I've been doing digital marketing for law firms for the past sixteen years. I've used every SEO out there. Jason is the best. He's the only person we recommend to our clients, and the only SEO we use for our projects."

—**Braden Pollack**, Founder of Legal Brand Marketing

"There is no one in the industry who knows SEO better than Jason. I highly recommend him to all of my clients simply because he is the best."

—**Jacob Malherbe**, Founder of X Social Media

"Jason is a clever marketer, a savvy businessman, and an all-around good guy. He's built an impressive company with over one hundred employees, and he's not showing any signs of slowing down."

—**Stephan Spencer**, coauthor of *The Art of SEO*

LAW FIRM SEO

EXPOSING THE GOOGLE ALGORITHM TO HELP YOU

🔍 **GET MORE CASES** 🎤

JASON HENNESSEY

LIONCREST
PUBLISHING

LAW FIRM SEO
Exposing the Google Algorithm to Help You Get More Cases

ISBN 978-1-5445-1937-1 *Hardcover*
      978-1-5445-1936-4 *Paperback*
      978-1-5445-1935-7 *Ebook*
      978-1-5445-1938-8 *Audiobook*

Contents

Foreword | x

Michael Mogill, Crisp Video, Founder and CEO

Introduction | 3

Chapter One | 11
What Is SEO?

CHAPTER TWO | 27
Behind the Scenes of the Google Algorithm

CHAPTER THREE | 41
The Three Main Components of SEO

CHAPTER FOUR | 55
Creating the Blueprint for Your Overall Web Strategy

CHAPTER FIVE | 67
Your Digital Marketing Team

CHAPTER SIX | 87
Tools to Help You Measure Success

CHAPTER SEVEN | 105
Content Strategy

CHAPTER EIGHT | 127

Increasing Your Website's Popularity One Link at a Time

CHAPTER NINE | 157

Technical SEO

CHAPTER TEN | 175

Getting onto Google Maps

CHAPTER ELEVEN | 191

The Importance of Photos and Videos in Your Strategy

CHAPTER TWELVE | 205

Turning Web Traffic into Cases

CHAPTER THIRTEEN | 225

Negative SEO

Conclusion | 241

Acknowledgments | 247

For my wife, Bridget,

and children, JJ, Zach, and Brooklynn,

who still have no idea what I do for a living,

but continuously support all

my crazy ideas.

"JASON HENNESSEY IS THE REAL DEAL. THE 1% OF SEO PROFESSIONALS WHO CAN MAKE A TRANSFORMATIONAL IMPACT IN YOUR LAW FIRM'S CASE VOLUME & REVENUE. FEW PEOPLE HAVE AS THOROUGH AN UNDERSTANDING OF AND PASSION TOWARDS SEO AS JASON. THE MAN IS LITERALLY OBSESSED WITH SEO AND HAS DEDICATED HIS LIFE TO IT."

MICHAEL MOGILL
CRISP VIDEO FOUNDER and CEO

BESTSELLING AUTHOR
THE GAME CHANGING ATTORNEY

Foreword

Michael Mogill, Crisp Video, Founder and CEO

The irony was not lost on me when Jason asked me to write the foreword for this book. It's no secret that I'm not very well-loved by many of the SEO agencies in the legal industry.

An unfortunate reality of SEO is its low barrier to entry. Anyone can take an online course, over the weekend, and then advertise themselves as an "expert" in SEO.

As a result, the legal industry is notoriously flooded with numerous fly-by-night SEO agencies and self-proclaimed SEO "gurus" who promise to get your law firm ranking on the first page of Google for meaningful keywords and then, unsurprisingly, fail to deliver.

For these reasons, among others, it's not uncommon for many attorneys to harbor at least some resentment towards SEO because they've been taken for a ride one too many times.

As the CEO of the nation's leading law-firm growth company, I've been outspoken in challenging SEO charlatans and have gone so far as to say that 99 percent of the SEO being done by these agencies isn't worth the investment, as it fails to move the needle in a meaningful way for most law firms.

Having helped over one thousand law firms drive nearly a billion dollars in revenue, I understand what it takes for law firms to stand out from the competition, attract the best cases, and become the obvious choice in their market. So, believe me when I tell you this: Jason Hennessey is the real deal—the 1 percent of SEO professionals who can make a transformational impact in your law firm's case volume and revenue. Few people have as thorough an understanding of and passion towards SEO as Jason. The man is literally obsessed with SEO and has dedicated his life to it.

I've always trusted professionals who practice what they preach, in their own organization, and Jason has not only helped many of the nation's fast-growing law firms generate millions in revenue through SEO, but he's also built many multimillion-dollar businesses of his own, leveraging the exact same strategies he outlines in this book.

If it's important for you to outrank your competition, drive more traffic to your website, get more leads, and, most importantly, sign more cases, SEO can help you achieve these goals.

Whether or not you're competing against hundreds or thousands of law firms in your market, simply dabbling with SEO won't get you results. The front page of Google only has so many spots, and if you aren't occupying at least one of them, your firm is at a competitive disadvantage.

With this book, Jason helps level the playing field for any law firm, regardless of size, market, or practice area. In its pages, you'll find an in-depth playbook on the most effective ways to drive real results for your law firm through SEO.

If you're ready to make a serious commitment to doing SEO the right way and learning from the best, the lessons you learn in this book will help you take your practice to the next level.

Best-Selling Author of
The Game Changing Attorney

SEO unleashes BUSINESS VALUE!

Introduction

"The jury returned a $25 million verdict in a case that came from a website lead," my client, who is a trial lawyer, told me over the phone.

As a search engine optimization (SEO) practitioner, that conversation stands out to me as one of the high points of my career—so far. It epitomizes the reason I've spent the last two decades reverse engineering Google's search algorithm: to connect lawyers with people who need them.

My client went on to say, "And that particular lead originated from a Google Organic Search, based on the SEO strategy, that you and your team have been implementing."

I could hear the excitement in his voice that day, and it went deeper than just the money. Not only had his investment in SEO paid off, with a major win for his law firm, but he had secured justice for a family that had suffered a terrible loss. Like David fighting Goliath, his firm had taken on a powerful insurance company and won.

When someone is injured or a loved one dies, there is no reversing the damage or bringing them back. But as a lawyer, you can do the next best thing and ensure that your client's family has financial stability. You can secure the funds that allow your client to pay off their home or send their kids to college. Victories like the one described above are what your hard work is all about.

Right now, there are potential clients who desperately need your services, but they can't find you. When they search for a lawyer, using Google, chances are your competitors are showing up above you and taking some of your market shares. Most of the time, it's not the best lawyers showing up in these searches; it's the best *marketers*. Specifically, digital marketers. SEO is their secret weapon.

SEO will increase the visibility of your website, so you attract more clients to your law firm. Unlike the broad, unfocused reach of a billboard, which does have its value, SEO empowers you to target exactly the types of clients you want, down to the specific keywords they're searching for on Google. One of these clients might be your next multimillion-dollar case.

Furthermore, SEO grows your website into a valuable business asset. By applying my proven SEO strategy, you can generate traffic worth thousands or millions of dollars in equivalent Google paid ads. Business brokers take into consideration a website's traffic and value, when prepping to sell your firm, making SEO a critical and worthwhile long-term investment. Done right, SEO will pay for itself and much more.

FORGET WHAT YOU THINK YOU KNOW ABOUT SEO

If you're reading this book, you've probably hired and fired half a dozen digital marketing agencies over the years. Despite all the fancy charts they presented, their efforts may never have translated into a meaningful increase in cases. In short, they may have promised the world, only to fail to deliver real results.

With so many self-proclaimed SEO experts out there, it's easy to get burned. You didn't know how to keep score then, but that's what this book will teach you. You'll have all the tools you need to hold a digital marketing team accountable or to manage your website's SEO yourself.

You'll learn how to:

- Understand SEO fundamentals
- Design and engineer your website's blueprint and architecture
- Recruit a digital marketing team and hold them accountable
- Measure the success of your SEO efforts
- Create a targeted content strategy
- Apply advanced SEO techniques to your website

I'm going to break down SEO, using simple, easy-to-understand explanations that address the specific marketing needs of law firms. If you're intimidated by SEO, don't be. Before working with my agency, many of my clients had gone to a bookstore, asked about SEO, and were pointed toward the computer-engineering section. They tentatively cracked open a book, only to be overwhelmed with technical jargon and more details than any law-firm owner or marketing director needs to know.

This isn't that kind of book. SEO doesn't have to be complicated, and you don't need to be a coder to understand and master it. In fact, I don't code myself.

WORKING IN SEO SINCE THE BEGINNING

SEO became a discipline in the late nineties, and by 2001, I had immersed myself in the field. Since then, I've spent most of my adult life reverse engineering Google's algorithm—figuring out exactly why Google ranks web pages the way it does. What does Google measure? What does it value? Why is one webpage ranked higher than another? What can you do to make your website reach more eyeballs? I found the answers.

All the information in this book is practical, not theoretical. It's based on my firsthand experience studying SEO in the legal vertical and working with some of the biggest law firms in America. Google doesn't publish the secrets behind their algorithm, so you won't find this information in universities. They certainly aren't teaching it in law school. It has taken many years of trial and error, growing many law firms' traffic and revenue, to develop proven SEO strategies that you can start implementing right away.

By the time you're done with this book, you'll truly understand what happens when you click "Search" on Google and how it impacts your website. Most importantly, I'm going to make it easy for you to implement my proven SEO strategy, dominate your market from a digital perspective, and sign more cases.

If you're ready to reach more clients, let's get started.

the SEO

Basics

CHAPTER ONE

What Is SEO?

Opening this book, you might have a rough idea of what SEO means. You know it's a series of actions you can proactively take to make your website more popular and your law firm more profitable. You may have paid experts to handle your SEO before, but perhaps their efforts didn't have a big impact. But one thing is certain: you are tired of wasting money on it.

I can tell you what SEO *doesn't* stand for: it's not the "Same Excuses Over and Over."

My kids would groan at the dad joke, but it's true. SEO has gotten a bad rap over the years. If you've worked with ineffective experts before, I understand why you'd feel wary of the subject, but done right, SEO is a worthwhile investment for your law firm that can deliver an exponential return on the value you put into it. If you own one of the larger firms in your area, SEO empowers you to continue dominating your market share. If you are right out of law school and just getting started, SEO allows you to gain market share from the bigger players in your city, often without them even realizing it.

SEO has existed only since the late nineties, and your competitors might not be leveraging it yet. Even the most successful law firms have just recently begun to shift some of their marketing budgets from television and billboards to SEO and digital. Therefore, becoming savvy in this new frontier can give you a significant competitive advantage over firms that aren't investing in their websites. Even though it's hard to remember what life was like before we had Google, the truth is that the internet is still young and evolving, and gaining an advantage in SEO can set your firm up for continued success for years to come.

Now is the time to take action, because the web is where you'll find your future clients. People don't watch television ads like they did a few decades ago. With streaming services, many people don't see ads at all. You need to meet your clients where they are: on the internet.

THE SEO BASICS

As I stated earlier, SEO stands for "search engine optimization." It's the practice of optimizing your website to increase your traffic and get in front of more targeted prospects at the precise time they are looking. Your law firm offers a solution, and your website connects prospects and their needs to your solution. SEO is just the means to strengthen that connection.

There are many search engines people use to find content on the internet, but in this book, I'll be focusing on the one with the largest audience: Google.

MARKET DOMINATION

Google dominates approximately 87 percent of the search engine market and web traffic. If a potential client searches for a law firm, about nine out of ten times, they're using Google. Google's algorithm factors in hundreds of variables, to rate and rank web pages, which it returns to users as search results in a matter of seconds. You can control some of these variables; others, you cannot.

Think of applying SEO principles to your website like maintaining a lawn. Let's assume your significant other is upset because they go into your backyard and see that your grass is turning brown. What can you do to make it greener? You can water it. You can put down fertilizer or soil. You can mow the grass once a week. These are all inputs you control to get your desired output—green grass. One thing you can't control is the sun, but you can adjust your behavior accordingly.

With SEO, just like maintaining your lawn, you will focus on the inputs you *can* control, to achieve your desired output of more traffic and leads. The three primary inputs you can control are: site integrity, relevancy, and popularity, which I'll cover in detail in Chapter 3. The uncontrollable element—the sun—is Google itself. Fortunately, while you can't control Google's algorithm, like the sun, you can predict how it will act.

All of Google's decisions reliably work toward two ends: making the company more profitable and providing a good user experience for its clients. Google wants people to continue using its search engine, which means it wants to promote content that answers users' questions and helps solve their problems. Seen from the user's perspective, the easier it is to find useful information on Google, the more you'll use it. And considering Google has an 87 percent market share, it has done a pretty good job of this. Seen from *your* perspective, the more user-friendly and helpful you make your website, generally speaking, the higher it will rank in the search results.

WHITE HAT VS. BLACK HAT SEO

Google's underlying algorithm produces its search results, and that algorithm changes constantly. Due to this constant change, it's critical to develop an SEO strategy that builds a lasting foundation of real value. You want your website to provide relevant information and solutions to problems, for Google to consistently rank your content and direct targeted traffic to your website.

To build a solid foundation, you want to engage in what are known as "white hat" SEO strategies, not "black hat" strategies. At its simplest, white hat SEO refers to strategies that adhere to the terms and conditions set by Google and other search engines. Black hat SEO, on the other hand, uses shortcuts and tricks to game the system, often by exploiting the algorithm to secure higher search rankings in a shorter period of time. However, in using these practices, you run the risk of getting your website penalized by Google. Yes, there really is a Google jail.

Generally speaking, black hat SEO can get you quick results, but whatever boost your website gains may potentially be short-lived. It would be a real shame to invest tens of thousands of dollars in SEO only to see your website get penalized the next time Google updates its algorithm. By "penalized," I mean removed from Google's listings completely. Black hat SEO is a flash in the pan, but white hat SEO, like the strategies I'll teach in this book, is sustainable and scalable. White hat strategies might take longer to implement and build upon, but the foundation you create for your website will be lasting and effective. In short, as a law firm, it's worth it to do SEO right.

A final word about black hat SEO: if it hasn't happened already, at some point, you will be approached by an SEO agency that promises you a fast path to the top of Google's search results. Just like with dieting and investments, if it sounds too good to be true, then it is. These firms are almost certainly using black hat techniques that can get your site penalized. Once that happens, you fire them and frantically look around for someone else who can help, while the agency goes off on its merry way, looking for the next law firm that will fall for its pitch.

A PROVEN STRATEGY

How can you make your website as user-friendly—and Google-friendly—as possible?

The proven strategy I teach starts with reverse engineering the websites that are currently ranking in the top three search positions in your market. You want to see what's working for your competitors and, later, apply those strengths to your website. You'll do this preliminary planning work before you even start thinking about the design for your website.

Combined with the SEO best practices and tools I'll introduce later in this book, your website can rise to the top of the search results and start generating more cases. However, you should know that SEO is a continued investment, not something you should start and stop. This isn't a one-and-done strategy—it's your website's forever strategy. Think of SEO like a retirement fund, where the more you invest over time, the more the value continues to compound, month over month. Pay-per-click, on the other hand, is more like day trading, where you get quick wins, but could be seen as a sunk cost. While they are different, both are great digital marketing strategies if executed correctly.

SEO Means More than Hiring a Web Developer

A common misconception among people new to SEO is to think, *I'll hire a web developer and pay them $5,000, one time, and that will be that.* But again—and this is a theme I will drive home throughout the book—SEO is an ongoing process. It requires more work than a single web developer doing a one-time audit of your website.

In my experience, most web developers and designers don't have SEO knowledge. You might even get emails from SEO "gurus" who claim that they can boost your website's search ranking for a flat fee, but be cautious. I get those emails, too. One-shot efforts may help, but my goal with this book is to educate and empower you so that you won't get taken advantage of.

I often hear from lawyers who tell me how their former SEO company would send them reports boasting about a lower bounce rate or higher conversion rate, yet they would leave the meeting perplexed. They didn't see an increase in the number of leads and signed cases, which in my opinion is the barometer of success. That's because an agency can spin any metric to sound like good news if you don't understand the technical terminology.

In an upcoming chapter, I'll explore how to decide whether you want to hire a digital marketing team in-house or work with an agency. Both have their advantages and disadvantages, depending on your needs. For now, know that a single web developer won't be able to fulfill all of your SEO needs.

How Much Does SEO Cost?

If a $5,000, one-time fee isn't going to cut it, how much *does* SEO cost?

The honest answer is that it costs as much as it needs to. It's impossible to say that one size fits all, because it depends on your market, your competition, and the search terms you are competing for. If your law firm operates in a market with a lot of competition, it will cost much more to compete and take market share than it would for a firm in a relatively smaller market.

You need to ask, "When I search Google for lawyers in my market today, who shows up?" The law firms currently ranking highest in your market are your competition, whether you like it or not, and they've had a head start. It's safe to assume they've invested in their SEO for several years already, and you will likely need to spend as much or more to take their market share. Alternatively, you might be able to use more advanced strategies to move the needle faster.

Some search terms may be so competitive that it's not even realistic to compete for them. For example, if someone offered me $5 million to rank number one on Google for the keyword "mesothelioma lawyer" in three months, I would have to tell them that it can't be done. That amount of money would not cover the work required to outrank the current leaders in that space within that time period. Google just doesn't work that way.

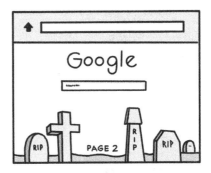

There are also domains that have so much popularity and authority that they're nearly impossible to outrank. For example, there isn't enough money in the world to try to compete with Wikipedia at this point. They've laid far too much groundwork and have millions of pages of content indexed on Google. Fortunately, you don't need to compete with Wikipedia—you only need to compete with other law firms in your specific market. Your law firm likely has several competitors that are taking SEO more seriously, and they're the ones fighting for the top three positions. That's the goal: to rank in the top three positions for your target keywords, or at the very least make it to the first page. As a popular SEO joke goes: "Where do you hide dead bodies? On the second page of Google."

My kids might cringe at that joke too, but statistics show that click-through rates drop dramatically the further down the search results you go. By the time a webpage gets pushed to the second page, the traffic drops to almost zero. Most users will rephrase their search query and get a fresh list of results instead of going to the second page, so it's critical to secure one of those top three spots.

Your competitors will play a significant role in how much you'll need to spend on SEO. Remember, they're the ones you need to outrank. However, if you operate in a smaller or less competitive market, SEO might cost less than you expect. For example, maybe your law firm does estate planning in Boca Raton, and you find that the market is wide open. Nobody has dominated that space online. In this scenario, a few thousand dollars per month might be enough to develop a strategy to secure the top search result for "Boca Raton estate planning lawyer" and start signing more cases and earning more revenue for your firm. Meanwhile, that same investment wouldn't be enough to impact a firm trying to compete for the keyword "Orlando personal injury lawyer," where you have some of the largest law firms in the country spending millions of dollars per month in marketing. Whatever you need to spend per month to compete in your market might seem high, but done right, SEO can deliver a significant return on your investment.

As a word of warning, if an SEO company offers you set pricing structures along the lines of "bronze, silver, or gold," I would be cautious. One size does not fit all, and to realistically cover the scope of the work required to compete, pricing expectations for SEO should be customized, depending on your market and competition.

Content Is Key to Your Strategy

A large part of this strategy will revolve around writing, optimizing, and publishing content to your website. Google values fresh content and even rewards sites that publish articles on a regular basis. I've seen sites lose their rankings and traffic by not being consistent with their content strategy. This is vital to maintain your positioning in the search engine results pages (SERPs).

Why the emphasis on content? I've always said, "Content is the food that Google eats."

Think about how Google makes its money: it serves ads on search results. If you're regularly publishing fresh content, you're providing more inventory for Google to serve additional ads and increase its profits. Google even has a "freshness algorithm," which promotes breaking news and current events, which will often jump to the top of the search results and temporarily rank above sites like Wikipedia.

By leveraging Google's algorithm and regularly publishing fresh content, you'll increase your search rankings and traffic, while building an asset that will exponentially grow over time.

SEO

→ Search engine optimization (SEO) is the art of making slight adjustments to your website to increase your positioning in the search engine results pages (SERPs).

→ It can be difficult and frustrating to differentiate the self-proclaimed experts who take advantage of people from the experienced and ethical professionals who demonstrate consistent, proven results.

→ SEO requires ongoing work to maintain and increase your Google ranking, so a single web developer or one-time solution may not cut it.

→ The cost of SEO depends on your market and competition. If your law firm operates in a competitive market, it will cost more to outrank the websites currently holding the top three positions.

→ Regularly publishing content is key to your SEO strategy and will help your website appear higher in search results.

Google

Q |

Google Search   I'm Feeling Lucky

CHAPTER TWO

Behind the Scenes of the Google Algorithm

What happens when you type a keyword or phrase into Google?

In a split second, the search engine returns a list of web pages relevant to the search query. But it's not magic returning the search results—it's a very complex and proprietary algorithm.

The algorithm scans all the pages in Google's index and decides which ones to display to you. It's the key to search rankings, and while the algorithm itself is complicated, here's a simple equation: a higher search ranking equals more traffic, leads, and revenue for your law firm.

In other words, if you understand how Google's algorithm works, you can leverage it to increase your rankings, sign more cases, and grow revenue for your firm.

THE ALGORITHM BREAKDOWN

Let's look at how Google's algorithm assigns value. Why does it rank one website higher than another?

When users have a good browsing experience, they stay on pages longer and view more ads. To that end, the algorithm values site elements that create a positive user experience, attract new viewers, and keep people browsing.

Google examines hundreds of variables and rewards websites that, among other things:

- Publish high-quality content on a regular basis
- Load quickly, preferably in under three seconds
- Deliver relevant information that satisfies the searcher's intent
- Offer a safe and secure browsing experience
- Use a responsive design that is user-friendly on both mobile and desktop

To rank pages in the SERPs and create its index, the algorithm looks at both the search term a user typed into Google and each page, which Google refers to as documents. Then, it asks questions, including:

- Do keywords from the search appear in the page's body copy, URL, or title tags?
- Is the page from a high-quality, trusted source?
- How old is the domain? When will it expire?
- How many links go to and from the page?
- How quickly did the page load?
- How much time do visitors spend on the webpage?

The algorithm considers the results and returns the pages that satisfy its criteria the best. As you'll see throughout this book, every aspect of your website factors into Google's algorithm to determine where your site ranks. Google is actually monitoring the user's experience and making adjustments to the search results daily. To rank highly, your website must meet the requirements listed above, deliver a great user experience, and continue to publish fresh content.

New Content Boosts Your Search Ranking

One of the best ways to get Google to crawl and index your website, more frequently, is by publishing new content. Every time you update your website by publishing new content, Google will visit it to see what has changed. Google maintains a carbon copy of the entire internet, and it's constantly "crawling" the web to keep its index up-to-date. This maintenance takes place behind the scenes, but what happens on the user's end?

When a Google search returns a list of pages, you see a snapshot of the internet, not a real-time scan. Google has already used software programs called spiders to crawl the web, follow links, collect information on pages, and create an index. Google uses a very complex algorithm to organize and rank the data, and then determines what will best satisfy your user intent for that particular search.

Google wants its snapshot to be as accurate to the real-time web as possible, but it can't monitor the entire web simultaneously. It prioritizes where to send its spiders by looking at how frequently a website gets updated.

Publishing new content is a powerful trigger that draws Google's spiders back to crawl your website again and again. It's why Google crawls websites like CNN.com constantly—the unending stream of news reports feeds the algorithm's hunger for content. In turn, Google ranks the site highly.

Your website probably won't be as active as CNN.com, but you should aim to post new content regularly. The algorithm wants to promote current, actively maintained websites, not sites that haven't been updated in years. If you add new pages frequently, it signals to Google that you take your website seriously, and you are rewarded with higher rankings and more traffic.

Technical Elements Make Your Website Crawlable

Publishing fresh content keeps you on Google's radar. It's critical to your overall web strategy, but your website won't benefit from your efforts if Google can't index your pages. Your website must also be technically sound, so Google's crawlers can scan it for information without any blockers.

What is Google looking at when it crawls your website?

A few of the most important technical elements that impact your Google search ranking include:

- Secure sockets layer (SSL) certificate, which indicates whether your website is secure or not
- Site speed, which is how fast your website loads
- Server-level performance, which is whether your pages load without error
- Domain age, which is the length of time your website has existed
- Domain expiration date, which is how much time remains before your website's registration expires
- Internal and external duplicate-content problems, which occur when a site plagiarizes content already indexed on Google

Technical Website Problems to Avoid

Many websites fail to rank highly because they have poor technical SEO—any element that impedes Google's ability to navigate the website. Some examples include:

- Broken internal links
- Linking out to pages that no longer exist
- Large, uncompressed images that slow down the website

These problems detract from your website's ranking, because they waste Google's resources. Google crawls the web, by traveling from link to link, so when it tries to follow a broken link, the algorithm doesn't gain any useful information. It hits a dead end. For example, if you've ever loaded a webpage and seen "404 Error," it means the page no longer exists. Google penalizes this inefficiency by docking the offending website's search ranking.

KNOW WHETHER A FEATURE
HELPS OR HURTS

It's easy to add a feature to your website, thinking it will improve the user experience and boost your search ranking, but sometimes these additions actually do just the opposite.

For example, chat services have become a popular feature on many law firms' websites. The feature works by opening a chat window on your website, where potential clients can ask questions about your firm. Sounds useful, right?

Yes, but only if it's a reputable chat service that's been implemented correctly. Many chat companies get paid for every chat they deliver. They're incentivized to get as many people using the feature as possible, so they'll make the chat window a large popup.

The problem is that large popups may be annoying, intrusive, and lead to a bad user experience—and Google knows this. Google calls features like this "intrusive interstitials," and may lower your search rankings.

Companies selling chat services or other features might not mention these potential issues, which may cause a Google penalty, so it's up to you to think about whether a feature helps or hurts the user experience. Don't get me wrong: there are plenty of chat services that adhere to Google's guidelines and provide amazing benefits and services. Some are much better than others, though, so do your homework before signing up for one of these services.

The Algorithm Assigns a PageRank

Google's algorithm examines hundreds of inputs, including the ones described above, and uses the data to calculate different scores. One of the most important is called "PageRank." PageRank—named after Larry Page, Google's co-founder alongside Sergey Brin—measures the popularity and relative value of a webpage, which factors into the webpage's overall placement in a list of search results.

PageRank estimates a webpage's importance by looking at the quality, relevancy, and number of inbound links pointing to it. For example, if a prestigious law school links to your firm's website, it will have a much greater impact than a link from your friend who owns a locksmith company. One is more popular and relevant to your website's content, and the other is not.

In the past, Google made PageRank visible so website owners could see how their webpages scored, but they have since obscured these scores. Fortunately, there are tools like Moz and Ahrefs that will approximate PageRank, so you can still get a good estimate of how your pages compare. Google's PageRank score ranges from zero to ten, becoming exponentially higher (a logarithmic scale) as the score rises, but many of the third-party tools function on a 1 to 100 scale.

Before you start making any changes to your website, I recommend using a tool to approximate its PageRank. This will give you a baseline for tracking improvements to your website's popularity and performance as you start to map out your SEO strategy.

EVERY ASPECT OF YOUR WEBSITE MATTERS

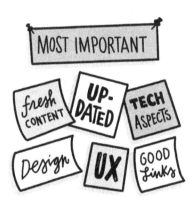

The most important thing you need to know about Google's algorithm, at this point, is that everything about your website matters. The content, update frequency, technical aspects, design, user experience, links, and more all contribute to how Google scores and ranks your webpages.

Remember, Google wants users to have a good experience and find the information they need, and it will reward websites that comply. That said, don't feel overwhelmed. By understanding how Google's algorithm works, you can be more proactive with your SEO strategy and get seen by as many potential clients as possible.

GOOGLE ALGORITHM

🔍 **TIPS AND TAKEAWAYS** 🎤

→ Google uses an algorithm that examines hundreds of variables to determine the best search results to return for any search term.

→ The search results you see aren't generated in real time, but are a snapshot of Google's index.

→ Google creates this index by constantly crawling the internet, using software programs called spiders.

→ Google's algorithm rewards websites that provide useful, relevant information and a user-friendly browsing experience.

→ Your website must be free of technical errors so Google can easily crawl it for new information.

→ Regularly publishing content will increase your rankings and traffic.

RELEVANCY

POPULARITY

INTEGRITY

CHAPTER THREE

The Three Main Components of SEO

While Google looks at hundreds of variables and crawls your website, everything its algorithm considers boils down to three questions: Is your content relevant to the particular search query? What is the popularity of your website? Is it secure, trustworthy, and accessible?

Google therefore uses three categories to rank your website: relevancy, popularity, and integrity.

RELEVANCY

Google wants to provide users with answers to their questions or solutions to their problems, as quickly as possible, which is why it measures the *relevancy* of webpages in relation to a search query. Relevancy simply measures the extent to which the content on a webpage addresses the user's intent for a specific keyword or phrase.

To determine relevancy, Google looks at many variables, including: how many times a keyword appears on a webpage, which is known as keyword density; how many other relevant websites link to that page; the keywords used in the anchor text of the link; and even behavioral patterns, such as how long users spend on the page after they conduct a search on Google.

For example, when someone clicks off of Google onto a page and stays there for six minutes, we can assume the content is interesting or useful to them, but if they quickly leave, after just a few seconds, and go back to the Google search results to click on another page, which is commonly referred to as "pogo sticking," the content probably didn't satisfy the user's intent for that particular search.

POPULARITY

To estimate the authority and importance of a website, Google takes *popularity* very seriously within its algorithm. As I described in the previous chapter, they use something called PageRank to rank webpages in their search engine results. PageRank is a link-analysis algorithm that uses a logarithmic scale to assign a value to every webpage, a.k.a. "document," on the internet.

The idea is that important websites are likely to receive more links from other websites. Not all links are equal though. For example, a link from a respected university would have a higher PageRank than a link originating from an obscure mommy blog. To prevent gaming the system, Google frowns upon link trading ("I'll link to your website if you link to mine, and we'll both get a boost."). Google values one-way links more than reciprocal links.

You'll want to build links naturally, by getting mentioned in the press, contributing content as a thought leader, on authoritative websites such as *Forbes*, *Entrepreneur*, and *Inc.*, or simply getting your law firm listed in a popular legal directory. We will cover this in greater detail in Chapter 8.

INTEGRITY

Technical SEO, or a website's *integrity*, is the third component Google considers when ranking webpages within their index. This is an area of SEO that can be intimidating but is crucial to the success of your digital marketing strategy.

Bottom line: you will need someone who knows technical SEO and can assess if there are any technical blockers preventing or impeding Google from accessing, crawling, and indexing your website. A website with high integrity will be secure, load quickly, and will follow best-practice, on-page technical SEO. It won't have broken links, internal or external duplicate content, unnecessary redirects, or issues preventing users from browsing on a tablet or a mobile device.

In short, a high-integrity website won't have any technical problems that detract from the user experience or make it difficult for Google to crawl its pages.

TOP-RANKING WEBSITES HAVE ALL THREE

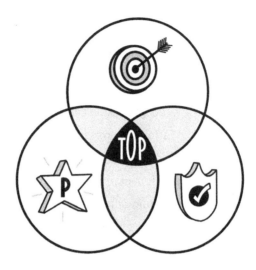

Relevancy, popularity, and integrity each play a critical role in your website's SEO success, but importantly, it's the *combination* of these three categories that will determine your website's search ranking, more than any single factor.

To demonstrate how all three are necessary to rank high on Google, let's imagine that you open your laptop and search for a "blueberry pancake recipe." The first page quickly returns ten excellent recipes, but you have your own recipe that you want to share. You create a webpage for your pancake recipe and wait to see what happens.

There's not much more you can do to make your recipe more relevant than any others, so you can check *relevancy* off your list. But even though your content is completely *relevant* to the search "blueberry pancake recipe," it's not *popular*. Nobody is visiting your website—yet.

You manage to get on the cooking show *Top Chef* and receive a ton of exposure. News stories and blogs link back to your website. *CNN* publishes an article declaring that you have the greatest blueberry pancake recipe in the world.

Now your website is extremely *popular* and *relevant*, but there's a problem: your server isn't set up to handle such a high volume of visitors. Your website slows to a crawl and goes down entirely. It lacks the *integrity* necessary to rank high on Google.

You fix your website's technical issues. Finally, your website has the SEO trifecta of relevancy, popularity, and integrity. Google recognizes these criteria, and before long, your recipe rises to the first page of search results for the term "blueberry pancake recipe," and you start receiving hundreds of thousands of visits to your website, each and every month.

Often, websites will compete for the top three positions in Google's search results—perhaps one page is more relevant to a keyword, but another page is more popular. Google will then use behavioral patterns and signals of the user conducting the search, to adjust the algorithm accordingly (e.g., how long do people stay on your blueberry pancake page after visiting from Google?), and it will place the webpage that consistently satisfies the user's intent higher in the search engine results pages (SERPs).

GOOGLE MUST CONSTANTLY OUTSMART MALICIOUS WEBSITES

You might be wondering, *Why doesn't Google simply rank the most popular, or the most relevant, websites the highest? Why take this more complicated, three-pronged approach?*

The answer is they used to, but over the years, their engineers have made necessary adjustments to their ranking signals. Google takes a sophisticated, complex approach to ranking webpages, because it must constantly outsmart individuals who try to take advantage of the algorithm (see black hat SEO in Chapter 1).

As an example, in 2010, an online eyeglass e-commerce website called DecorMyEyes was accused of treating customers horribly, failing to ship orders, and outright stealing money. As you can imagine, the company received a large amount of bad press, but this negative attention started to benefit the website in terms of Google rankings and traffic. The company's owner knew that the more press the company received and the more links from trusted sources pointed back to his website, the higher the website would rank on Google and the more money he would make.

At the time, Google's algorithm put more emphasis on a website's popularity as a ranking signal, without giving due consideration to other factors, like the company's reputation or the sentiment of the press. So when *The New York Times* wrote an article condemning the company, the algorithm misinterpreted it as a highly reputable media source vouching for the company by way of a link. The more negative attention and links the company earned from trusted sources, the higher they ranked on Google, for competitive keywords, which increased their rankings, traffic, and sales.

Google then changed its algorithm to detract from companies with poor reputations, and the algorithm has only grown more sophisticated over the years, making it harder for people to manipulate it. The change in the algorithm is both a blessing and a curse. It's a blessing, because malicious SEO practitioners now have a much harder time gaming the system. It's also a curse, because the algorithm makes it more complicated, and the obfuscation on Google's part about how it works makes it more difficult to raise the visibility of your website. But that's why I wrote this book: to help you leverage and understand it.

HOW OFTEN DOES GOOGLE'S ALGORITHM CHANGE?

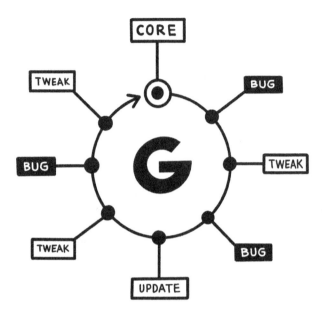

The story above is just one example of Google updating its algorithm to work more efficiently, produce better results, or combat manipulation, but these kinds of changes happen all the time.

A month rarely passes without an update being made, and while many are simple bug fixes or minor algorithm tweaks, every once in a while, Google releases a significant update—commonly referred to as a "core update"—that shakes the SEO world. What kind of changes does Google make?

One of the most notable core updates Google made to its algorithm was called Panda. Released in 2011, Panda aimed to reduce the amount of thin, low-quality content being published on the internet. Prior to the update, the algorithm relied too heavily on a site's authority without taking into consideration the relevancy and quality of the content. For example, highly authoritative and popular publishers like *Huffington Post* would put up short webpages for common search terms, such as "when does the Super Bowl start?"

The webpage would contain short, thin content, and the overall website wasn't relevant to football, and yet Google found these pages ranking higher than the NFL itself. Panda fixed the issue by rewarding high-quality content that kept visitors' attention for longer, and pushing down thin, irrelevant pages.

However, it didn't take long until Google required another update to combat bad behavior. After Panda, the Penguin update came out, in 2012, to address unnatural and artificial link-building techniques that manipulate search results. This update was aimed at decreasing search-engine rankings of websites that violated Google's webmaster guidelines.

Before Penguin, people would successfully use many spammy link-building strategies. One strategy would be to find a forum or blog and leave a spammy comment, with a link back to their website. For example, you might be on a forum about Ferraris when you suddenly see a comment advertising a criminal defense lawyer in Miami, with a link to their website. This strategy worked, because in crawling the Ferrari forum, Google would follow the link and boost the popularity of the defense lawyer's website, based upon the authority of the website and the anchor text used in that link, but not necessarily the relevancy. Google fixed the problem with the Penguin update, by penalizing websites that engaged in this type of activity.

"With so many updates, won't I need to constantly adjust my website and SEO strategy?" you might ask.

The answer is no, not fundamentally. SEO requires ongoing effort, as you publish new content and build new links, but the good news is that if you follow the strategy in this book and generally adhere to white hat SEO practices (i.e., you play by Google's rules), your rankings and traffic will continue to grow and compound exponentially, month over month, regardless of whatever changes Google makes.

Remember, at the end of the day, Google is an internet search engine that uses a proprietary algorithm designed to retrieve and order search results, to provide the most relevant and dependable sources of data possible. Google just wants to provide the best possible user experience, which will keep people coming back; obviously, it does a good job, since it controls 87 percent of the market share and has a market cap of over $1 trillion. In summary, as long as your website adheres to the guidelines referenced in this chapter, you should have nothing to worry about.

RELEVANCY, POPULARITY, AND INTEGRITY

➜ Relevancy measures the degree to which the content on a webpage relates to a Google user's search term.

➜ Popularity is determined by how many links point back to a webpage, and the authority of those originating websites.

➜ Integrity refers to a website's technical components, including page speed, crawlability, mobile responsiveness, and the lack or presence of broken links, among other things.

➜ High-ranking websites will have all three components: relevancy, popularity, and integrity.

➜ Google constantly updates its algorithm to counteract attempts to manipulate or cheat the ranking system.

➜ Google wants your website to be fast, easy to use, and informative. As long as you practice an ongoing SEO strategy that creates a good user experience and follows Google's rules, like the one in this book, your website should be able to keep up with any algorithm changes.

SEO
BLUEPRINT

CHAPTER FOUR

Creating the Blueprint for Your Overall Web Strategy

By now, you might be eager to dive into more fun and familiar territory, like the colors and logo of your website's design, but design comes way down the line. Website design is like home decorating— we're still architecting the blueprint. Just like you would never build a house without laying a foundation, you don't want to build a website without first creating your strategy, either.

You've been operating without a plan, until now, but it's time to change that. At this point in the process, you'll create your SEO roadmap and preplan your content strategy and website architecture.

Before creating your strategy, I want to share the top four reasons SEO efforts fail to produce results. These are traps you can easily avoid—if you know what to expect.

The first and most common reason for failure is treating SEO like a one-and-done project. People who make this mistake typically hire a web designer or developer, who builds them a beautiful website and then checks SEO off of their list. However, while most web designers and developers may have a basic understanding of SEO, generally speaking SEO is probably not their true passion or core competency. They might apply some of the SEO 101 basics to your website and tell you that it is good to go, but in reality, they are just 10 percent of the way there. As I've mentioned in previous chapters, SEO requires ongoing effort: regular content publishing, link building, and technical maintenance to stay competitive in your market.

The second mistake people make is assuming they need a blog on their website and outsourcing it with no strategy. You might hire a content writer to create blog posts and pay them $50 per weekly post. The problem is that these writers often work in a silo and lack focus. Their blog posts cover a random assortment of topics, chosen by them, which may even hurt you more than help you. Even worse, a content writer might plagiarize content, which could get your website algorithmically filtered or penalized. In short, regularly publishing content is good, but only if you have a clearly defined strategy. The strategy should take into consideration what content you've already published on your website and the gaps for attracting your target audience with new content.

The third mistake that lawyers often make is treating SEO like pay-per-click advertising, which can be turned on, completely changed, and turned off at a moment's notice. Unfortunately, SEO strategies require planning and preparation, along with continuous effort to research, write, optimize, and publish targeted content, while increasing the popularity of those pages, with link building, to move them closer to the first page of Google. If you start an SEO campaign and then abruptly stop, you lose all of the momentum that you had been building, and most of your content and investment will remain indexed on the fifth page of Google, or greater.

Lastly, SEO efforts can fail if you engage an SEO company that doesn't have experience working with lawyers and may deploy unproven strategies. How can you tell an unproven strategy from a proven one?

A proven strategy will be customized to your law firm's goals and will clearly lay out how the company intends to increase traffic to your website using practices that have been effective for some of their other lawyer clients. If the SEO company tries to sell you a generic bill of goods—a one-size-fits-all solution—their strategy will likely fail to produce results. A true, diehard SEO expert will create a personalized strategy, laid out in a spreadsheet, that breaks down every aspect of your website's technical architecture and includes content strategy and silos, URL structure, header tags, meta descriptions, internal-link planning, structured markup, pillar pages, and more.

PLANNING YOUR PILLAR PAGES

At the top of your strategy checklist should be planning your pillar pages. A pillar page is a webpage focused broadly on a single topic from which related, in-depth pages—called "cluster content"—branch out. Pillar pages could range from a thousand words to ten thousand words, depending on how competitive that keyword or phrase is.

Using pillar pages is a good strategy that silos and organizes your information by topic, in a way that makes it easy for visitors to navigate, and equally easy for Google to associate relevance while crawling and indexing. Remember, crawlability is a critical component to the success of your SEO campaign and site integrity, which can have a major impact on whether or not your site ranks high in search results.

To demonstrate how a pillar page works, imagine that you're an immigration lawyer. One pillar page you might want to create would be about how to get a visa to come work in the United States. This page would then link to subtopic pages that cover related topics and questions, such as "What is an H-1B visa?", "How long does an H-1B last?", and "What is the difference between an H-1 and an H-1B?" The pillar page would strategically and internally link to each of these subpages, using keyword anchor text to strengthen that content silo.

As another example, look at how Wikipedia structures its website. If you go to the Wikipedia page for baseball (the pillar page), you'll find a link to a subpage for batting. The batting page then introduces baserunners, and from baserunners you can link to a page about the fielder's choice. This branching structure continues deeper and deeper to related content, but it all connects back to the pillar page for baseball and, again, strengthens that content silo. The goal is to build the most authoritative resource about a particular subject, which Wikipedia has been doing for years. This is no different from what you're trying to do with your law firm and your digital marketing strategy.

A critical part of your content strategy will be deciding what pillar-page topics will help you connect with your target audience. You'll want to ask yourself:

- What topics are important to our clients?
- What questions are potential clients asking in Google searches?
- Who is already ranking on Google for these searches, and what does their content look like?
- What information does the user need to know?
- Do we have different geographic locations that need their own practice-area pages?
- What does the search volume and competition look like?

The benefit of preplanning your pillar pages and content strategy is that you can attract, inform, and educate targeted prospects who are looking for your specific services, at the exact moment they are ready to retain an attorney. You'll be able to measure your organic traffic for chosen keywords in Analytics, after Google crawls and indexes your content, and then you can re-optimize your content to increase your rankings and traffic, while signing more cases.

STUDY YOUR COMPETITORS

To figure out what topics you want for your pillar pages, an excellent place to start is by studying your top competitors. If their websites are ranking at the top of Google searches, they're doing something right. Google is looking at their webpage as some of the most relevant and authoritative documents for this particular search query, and there are insights and patterns that you or your content team can study when writing and publishing your content.

Your first step should be to find out who ranks at the top of Google searches for your market—they're your main SEO competition. Identifying your competition is as easy as Googling your law firm's practice area and location. If you're a personal injury lawyer in Miami, for example, run a search for that and see who comes up.

Creating the Blueprint for Your Overall Web Strategy

Be aware, however: one thing to take into consideration is that the big spenders you recognize from television and billboards may not be using best practices with their technical SEO, but may still be ranking. They've likely built up years of natural links, from their advertising and community involvement, resulting in popularity superseding the technical aspects of their website. This goes to show how much weight Google places on links and popularity within the Google algorithm.

Don't be surprised to find that newer firms are also top ranking for some of these searches—this is where recent law school graduates tend to have an advantage. Lawyers who have been in the market for a long time and have already built a brand may be susceptible to complacency, whereas a new lawyer with a more sophisticated SEO strategy can swoop in and start to take away some of their online market shares.

Reverse Engineering Your Competitors' Strategies

Once you have a list of your competitors, it's time to reverse engineer their SEO strategy. Start by crawling their websites, using tools like Screaming Frog SEO Spider, Ahrefs, or Semrush (all of which I'll describe in greater detail in Chapter 6).

These tools will provide insights and answer questions like: "What keywords does the website rank for?" and "What does their backlink profile look like?" Also, pay attention to how the websites are technically structured, how pages link together, and how URLs are formatted. I suggest analyzing your top three competitors and making a spreadsheet with the following information:

- Number of total pages indexed on Google
- Number of organic keywords they are ranking for on Google, using Semrush
- Estimated organic traffic cost, using Semrush
- Estimated branded and non-branded traffic, using Semrush
- Domain Rating (often abbreviated online and in SEO literature as DR), using Ahrefs
- Total number of referring domains, sorted by highest DR to lowest DR, using Ahrefs
- Top pages and all associated ranking keywords for each page, using Ahrefs

This information can inform your strategy, as you decide which keywords your website should include and where you should direct your link-building efforts, among other choices.

BASELINE Metrics

As you're studying your competitors' websites, compare them to your own. You want to set baseline metrics for measuring progress later. For example, look at how many pages Google has indexed on your website versus your competitors'. You can do this by using the following search operator on a Google search: **site:yourdomain.com**. By conducting this search on Google, it will report back how many pages you have indexed. Be sure to do this same exercise for all of your competition to get a comparison. If you have 55 pages indexed on Google, and your largest competitor has 5,500 pages indexed on Google, then you may have some catching up to do.

When analyzing your website, you want to compare the number of HTML pages you have on your server to the number of pages indexed on Google. If you have more pages indexed on Google, there might be some technical issues that you need to fix, or you may have been hacked.

Barring a situation where you've been hacked, generally speaking the more unique pages you have indexed on Google, the better. There are only two ways to increase organic traffic to a website from an SEO perspective: you can publish more content, which will rank for more keywords, or you can push legacy pages higher in the SERPs with link-building strategies. For example, if you are ranking on the top of page two for a keyword that has five thousand searches per month, pushing your site to the first page of Google would increase your impressions, click-throughs, and traffic.

Creating the high-level blueprint for your strategy might not be as exciting as designing the look and feel of your website, but it's as necessary a first step as architecting a building before breaking ground. If you put in the time now to plan your pillar pages, study the competition, set baseline metrics and goals, and reverse engineer winning strategies, you'll set yourself up for long-term SEO success.

STRATEGY BLUEPRINT

Q TIPS AND TAKEAWAYS 🎤

→ Create your personalized SEO strategy blueprint before building your website.

→ Plan out your pillar pages and the more in-depth subpages that will link to them.

→ Identify the top competitors in your market.

→ Study your competitors' websites, using tools like Screaming Frog SEO Spider, Ahrefs, and Semrush. Pay attention to their content strategy, ranking keywords, backlinks, and more.

→ Reverse engineer your competitors' strategies so you can dominate your market and take more digital market share.

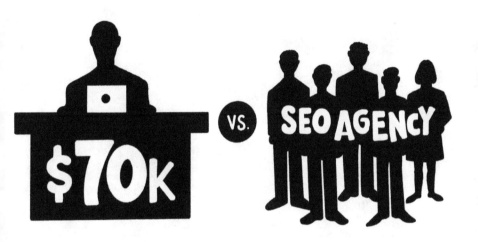

CHAPTER FIVE

Your Digital Marketing Team

You now understand the basics of SEO and have begun to draft a high-level strategy that will help boost your website's search ranking and start generating more revenue for your firm. You can get the ball rolling yourself, but as a lawyer, your passion probably isn't writing content or building links—it's practicing law. Your time is better spent, and probably more profitable, doing what you do best, which means your next step is hiring a team to develop and execute the SEO strategy. Now that you are armed with the knowledge from this book, you are empowered to make the right decision.

You've reached a fork in the road with two options: build an in-house digital marketing team, or hire an external agency. Both choices have pros and cons, so the real question is which is right for your law firm?

That's the question this chapter will answer. No matter which path you go down, you'll also need to know how to hold your digital marketing team accountable. So many law firms have been burned by the agency or so-called specialist they hired to manage their SEO.

They charge thousands of dollars a month and, in most cases, fail to deliver results, but that cycle ends now.

By the time you're finished with this chapter, you'll know:

- Whether your law firm needs an in-house team or an external agency
- The job titles and competencies you want for your digital marketing team
- How to write a compelling job description that attracts top talent
- How to define and measure success

You'll have all the tools you need to find the perfect digital marketing team for your firm.

IN-HOUSE OR AGENCY?

Building an in-house SEO team has many benefits, including control over your data, over whom you choose to hire, and over which person does what job, among other considerations. However, unless your law firm does a volume of business that justifies spending upwards of $25,000 per month on an in-house marketing team, you'll likely be better served by hiring an outside agency.

Now, hold on, Jason, you might be thinking. *Why can't I hire one salaried SEO specialist for $70,000 a year to do all the work?*

You can, but the reality is that a single person won't have all of the proficiencies and the array of talents needed to do an exceptional job. They probably won't be a great content writer *and* a technical SEO expert *and* a link-building specialist *and*—you get the idea. Most likely, they'll do a lackluster job and fail to produce strong results. I would argue that you might be setting them up to fail, and not even know it. In the same way you wouldn't hire one person to build your house—you'd hire an architect, an electrician, a plumber, and so on— you shouldn't hire a single person to manage and execute your overall SEO strategy.

A good digital marketing agency will have people who specialize in all the areas you need, and for their monthly fee—five figures is reasonable for a midsized law firm—you'll have access to them all. That price tag might sound expensive, until you consider the astronomically higher cost of hiring all those specialists separately, building the strategy yourself, and then micromanaging them. For these reasons, working with a reputable agency that has a large team and a proven strategy may be the best choice for most law firms. It keeps costs reasonable, while still granting you access to top talent who are experts in their fields, not to mention the savings of thousands of dollars in licenses and tools that are necessary to develop, monitor, and execute the strategy.

As a word of warning, if an agency gives you a low quote—let's say $1,500 per month—that might be a red flag. For such a low cost, there's no way the agency can devote enough resources to your SEO to make a difference and still make a profit. Think about all of the SEO efforts I've discussed so far in this book, and now consider how many hours that $1,500 will get you. Heck, I even pay interns more than that at my agency. The two figures—the time required and the time afforded—do not add up with such a low budget and will, most likely, not produce results.

Here's what tends to happen with cheap agencies: several months may pass with little to no results. The law firm hiring the agency typically gets frustrated and puts pressure on the agency to start producing return on investment (ROI). The agency, still with too few resources to make a real impact, might take shortcuts, perhaps even turning to black hat SEO strategies to show short-term gains.

Before long, Google catches on to these tactics, which may go against Google's webmaster guidelines, and penalizes your website.

In this way, opting for a cheap agency may not only fail to produce results, but it can actually do more harm than good. And this, my friends, is why SEOs have such a bad rep. Welcome to my world!

KEY ROLES ON A DIGITAL MARKETING TEAM

Whether you're building your own digital marketing team or hiring an external one, it's important to know which roles should be present. What does the perfect digital marketing team look like, and why does it look that way?

At the least, a strong digital marketing team should include the following roles:

- Marketing director
- Digital marketing manager
- Copywriter

- Technical SEO lead
- Web Developer
- Public relations specialist
- Link building and outreach specialist
- Social media manager
- Paid media strategist
- Graphic designer
- Video editor
- Data Analyst

Let's go through each role, from the perspective of hiring a digital marketing team.

Marketing Director

Your law firm might be investing in digital marketing, while also doing community outreach, advertising on the radio, and putting up billboards in your city, and someone needs to be the ringleader of these activities. That person is a marketing director—the individual who oversees and coordinates all of your various marketing efforts, while budgeting, tracking, and attributing your return on ad spend for each marketing channel. If you hire an external digital marketing agency, you might have a marketing director on your staff who manages the relationship with your digital marketing agency directly, or manages an internal digital marketing manager who works with the agency and holds them accountable.

Digital Marketing Manager

The digital marketing manager, as the name suggests, focuses solely on your digital efforts. The digital marketing manager is the liaison between the digital marketing team and your law firm's marketing director. This person also manages the other roles on the digital marketing team.

Larger law firms might have a digital marketing manager on staff who specializes in pay-per-click advertising, for example, but not SEO. In this case, they consider working with an SEO agency, because SEO is not their skillset or core competency. The digital marketing manager would be responsible for attending meetings with the agency, reviewing the content they produce, and generally making sure the agency produces results.

Copywriter

The new webpages you'll create need clear, concise information that speaks to your target audience, and the person with the skillset to do that is a copywriter. While their job title is "copywriter," you ideally want someone whose talents also include storytelling, or you'll want to hire two people with different skillsets.

The most compelling websites do more than regurgitate dry facts. They tell a story in a way that your potential clients can relate to, and the copywriter is responsible for telling the story of your law firm. In shaping that story, think about the problems you solve for your clients and the challenges they have faced. What was your role in their legal triumphs?

Too many law firms simply slap their partners' faces on their homepage and list the awards they've won, but that won't make potential clients pick up the phone. If someone has been injured in a car accident or, worse, lost a loved one, for example, they aren't thinking about you; they're thinking about themselves. They're thinking, *I'm going to be out of work for a year. How am I going to pay my bills? I'm a stay-at-home mom; how am I going to be able to pay the mortgage now?* A good copywriter will capture this emotion and be able to tell a compelling story about your law firm's mission, while getting into the mental psyche of the user, with empathy towards their situation.

Technical SEO Lead

On any SEO team, you'll also want to have someone who specializes in technical issues. They're the person who will fix page-speed problems, develop internal-linking strategies, optimize content and source code using schema markup, and monitor tools like Google Search Console to continuously identify and fix any and all technical errors. It's important that the technical SEO lead is proactive and not reactive to your overall strategy. At the same time, they should look for new opportunities to leverage your web assets while increasing your rankings and traffic. They will also be your go-to when Google releases an algorithmic update that shakes up the SERPs.

Web Developer

The web developer works on the website to implement the recommendations of the technical analyst. They typically have HTML, CSS, PHP, JavaScript, and WordPress experience. I recommend avoiding platforms like Wix and Squarespace for your website, because they give you less control over your website's functionality, which may impede your efforts when you want to use more-advanced SEO practices. The web developer should also know how to speed up the performance, handle backend programming, deal with the server, fix broken links, and eliminate unnecessary redirects, among other website responsibilities.

Public Relations Specialist

The public relations specialist interacts with the media and builds relationships with reporters, writers, and publications. They build the attorney's public image as a subject matter expert, set up speaking engagements, arrange podcast opportunities, and pitch the attorney for contributor columns on sites like *Forbes, Inc.*, and *Entrepreneur*. It's important that the public relations specialist is able to work with the media on different story angles, land featured articles, and get quotes placed with reputable media platforms, including online, print, podcasts, television, and more.

Link Building and Outreach Specialist

Your digital marketing team should also include someone responsible for outreach and link building. They'll perform some of the reverse-engineering work discussed in the previous chapter, to ensure that your website has as many or more quality links as your competitors. They'll strategically add your law firm to legal directories, coordinate with the copywriter to distribute press releases that generate news links, build relationships with bloggers for guest-blog-post opportunities, and work with the copywriter to create assets they can use in their outreach initiatives to attract more links and boost the authority of the website.

Social Media Manager

A strong digital marketing team will also have a social media manager who handles all organic social media growth. This is one role that benefits from being part of your internal team instead of part of the agency you hire, and that's because social media engagement requires an in-office presence. You want someone who understands the local market and can capture the essence of life at your law firm, interact with clients, understand your culture, and create engagement with your followers. While you can hire an agency to help develop a strategy, in my experience, for this position it makes more sense to have someone who works in-house at the law firm.

Paid Media Strategist

The paid media strategist has a different skillset than the social media manager, in that they work with paid ad campaigns, not on organic social activity. They know how to build pay-per-click campaigns on Google, Bing, YouTube, and other search engines. The paid media strategist also sets up paid campaigns and retargeting campaigns, on Facebook and other social media channels. They should understand how to modify campaigns, on a daily basis, to maximize impact, and how to calculate the cost per signed case, so you know exactly what you're getting for your paid media budget.

Graphic Designer

Text only makes up part of your website's content, which is why you'll also want a graphic designer on the team. This person might be an employee of the digital marketing agency or work on a freelance basis as needed. Chances are, however, that you'll need their services more than you expect. Regularly publishing content requires graphics for blog posts, social media, infographics, pillar pages, subtopic pages, and even YouTube thumbnails.

Video Editor

Video is more prevalent, and effective at generating leads, than ever before, so having a video editor on hand is as important as the graphic designer. Occasionally, these two skillsets overlap, but you might need to hire individuals for each role. You'll want to publish videos to You-Tube as well as other video-hosting websites, because each instance counts as a link pointing back to your website. Plus, having video on the tops of your important pages will keep people on the page longer and increase the chances of converting that traffic to leads.

Data Analyst

Lastly, your team should have a data analyst in charge of tracking data and making sure leads get attributed to the right sources. If your law firm spends money on both pay-per-click ads and SEO, you need a way to discern which efforts are producing results. Are you getting more leads from pay-per-click or from SEO? You won't know what works, without data, so your analyst plays a critical role in gauging the effectiveness of your overall digital marketing investment. The analyst defines and measures success, handles conversion-rate optimization, runs split tests to compare different design options, and creates reports that keep you apprised of progress and your return on investment.

THE RIGHT TEAM FOR YOUR LAW FIRM

Choosing whether to build your own digital marketing team or hire an agency is a big decision, but again, for most law firms, going with an agency will most likely be the best economical and effective solution. Generally speaking, for the same price it would take to hire just a single competent member of an in-house team, you gain access to the full expertise of an agency with dozens or more professionals who are experts in their fields.

At the very least, you'll want your digital marketing team to have the roles described above. Some of these roles might overlap—for example, it's possible (but rare) to find someone who's knowledgeable in both technical SEO and web development. In most cases, these are very different skillsets. The important thing to remember is that these skillsets should both be represented on your digital marketing team.

To make sure you're hiring the right agency for your law firm, do your due diligence. Start with the following actions:

- Ask the agency if they work with other law firms and understand the legal marketing space.
- Use the tools that I've mentioned, in earlier chapters, to see if their SEO has been effective.
- Speak with references.
- Ask to speak to the last law firm that fired them. It will be interesting to see how they answer that question.
- Ask what roles the team will include, and who does what. Make sure they have most of the talent and skills previously mentioned in this chapter.

- Does the agency have a graphic designer? Is someone proficient in technical SEO? What does their content team look like? Do they even have a content team? You'd be surprised; there are many agencies that don't offer copywriting as a service.
- Ask them to send examples of their work. Read the examples, and then ask yourself if you would feel comfortable hiring the firm that they wrote the copy for.

Do your due diligence, because unscrupulous SEO companies may be counting on the fact that most lawyers don't understand SEO and how it works. But now, you're armed with the knowledge you need to never be taken advantage of again.

If your budget limits you to hiring a small agency that might only assign a single person to your firm, you might be better off skipping the middleman and building your own internal team of one or two people. Again, a single person won't excel at a huge variety of skills, so this isn't an ideal scenario, but it is still more than many of your competitors are doing.

LOOK FOR TALENT BEYOND YOUR BACKYARD

Once upon a time, working as a team meant gathering in the same office every day. The necessity of physical proximity limited your hiring choices to only the people willing to make the commute. Being headquartered in a small town also meant a small talent pool, but those days are over.

With virtual technology and video chats, you can hire digital marketing professionals from anywhere in the country, or even the world. There's no reason to limit yourself to local talent when you could have a marketing director in one state and a graphic designer in another, with little to no problem. In fact, that's how I've built my agency. My team works together remotely, with over a hundred people collaborating from around the globe.

In this way, technology has allowed us to recruit some of the smartest minds in digital marketing regardless of where they are located.

Your Digital Marketing Team

HOLDING YOUR TEAM ACCOUNTABLE

Once you've found the right digital marketing team, your next challenge will be to hold them accountable. Your ability to hold people accountable depends entirely on you being aware of what they're doing and understanding the outcomes. This means asking yourself the following questions:

- Is the digital marketing team publishing content on a regular basis?
- Am I satisfied with the content they're putting out?
- If I were a potential client of the law firm, would I hire my firm based on what I'm seeing?

If the answer to any of these questions is "no," you probably want to make adjustments quickly before the digital marketing team continues to go down this path for months on end. The most successful law firms that are marketing online have somebody at the firm, whether the owner, lawyer, digital marketing manager, or another team member, working closely with the agency and providing feedback. The agency is only going to be as successful as how involved you are with them. You might consider giving this book to your director of marketing so they can hold the agency accountable.

As you guide your digital marketing team's efforts, always focus on putting your clients and potential clients first. If you aren't getting results, the problem might not be your team's actions but the direction and subject of the content itself. Start by stepping into your clients' shoes. Your website should answer the questions they might have. In other words, try to separate yourself from what you already

know and instead think about what your *clients* need to know. These are the topics and questions you want to address that will boost your traffic and increase the number of potential clients calling your office.

Remember, you are not writing to another lawyer. In fact, it's just the opposite. When writing your content, I recommend expressing sympathy for your clients, with your messaging and writing, at an eighth-grade reading level. The agency doesn't need lawyers on staff to write your content; however, they should be aware of legal ethics and professional responsibility in your state.

You Can't Control What You Don't Understand

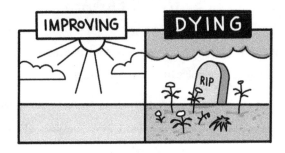

As I described in Chapter 1, SEO is like trying to turn the grass in your yard green. You can control certain inputs, like how much you water the grass and whether you put down fertilizer, but you can't control the sun, which is essential to getting the output of green grass. In the same way, you can control your SEO inputs, like link building and content creation, but you can't control Google's algorithm to get the output of higher search rankings and more traffic to your website. However, both the sun and Google's algorithms are predictable, based on patterns, historical data, and insights.

And here's one more key part to the equation: to determine if your yard care is working, you need to monitor the grass and understand whether it's improving or dying. It's the same with SEO.

When you understand *what* work your digital marketing team is doing and *why* they're doing it, you can also understand and predict their results. You can compare those results to the baseline to determine whether your team has been successful, and in doing so, you can hold them accountable. You can't measure what you don't understand, so choosing the right team for your law firm, and understanding their efforts yourself, are critical to seeing positive SEO outcomes.

DIGITAL MARKETING TEAM

Q TIPS AND TAKEAWAYS 🎤

→ You have the option to either build your own in-house digital marketing team or hire an outside agency.

→ For most law firms, it probably makes financial sense to hire an agency. You can pay much less than it would cost to build an in-house team, and you'll still have access to a wide range of experts in their specific fields.

→ A great SEO team needs people to write content, manage technical SEO aspects, and analyze the results.

→ Your digital marketing team should include the following roles: marketing director, digital marketing manager, copywriter, technical SEO lead, web developer, public relations specialist, link building and outreach specialist, social media manager, paid media strategist, graphic designer, video editor, and data analyst.

→ Once you've hired your team, hold them accountable. You can't control what you don't understand, so it's important to follow the reports, review their work yourself, and monitor progress over time.

SEO

TOOLS

CHAPTER SIX

Tools to Help You Measure Success

In the same way you can't know that your grass is getting greener without looking at it, you won't know if your SEO efforts are working without measuring the results. For that, you need the tools I'll describe in this chapter.

These tools can provide insights on website performance, site integrity, keyword research, content strategy, link analysis, traffic monitoring, and more, all of which give you a deeper understanding of how Google evaluates your website and indexes it within the search engine result pages (SERPs).

GOOGLE IS YOUR MOST POWERFUL TOOL

Dozens of tools exist to help you organize your SEO activity, measure performance, and manage your website, but perhaps the strongest tool of all is Google itself.

Search Operators

One of the most powerful tools for finding the information you need on Google is the search operator. Google allows you to use short commands called "search operators" to refine your search queries, so you can find exactly what you're looking for. They are commands that tell Google how to include, exclude, and sort its data.

Here are a few examples of the most useful operators:

Site:

The **site:** search operator will give you a lot of useful insights when analyzing your website against your competition. Not only will this reveal how many pages of content your website has indexed on Google, but it will also help you forensically audit technical issues with your site. This is where SEO starts to become fun. Go to Google, type **site:yourdomain.com** into the search bar, and press enter. After the results populate, you should see the word "About" with a number next to it. This is a good estimate of the number of pages your domain has indexed on Google. Now do the same exercise using your competitors' websites. If they have 5,000 pages of content indexed and you only have 270 indexed, you may have some catching up to do in terms of content creation.

The **site:** search operator is also a clever way to forensically look for technical problems and opportunities on your website. For example, if you do a **site:yourdomain.com** search on Google and find that there are 10,000 pages of content indexed, but you know you should have only a few hundred pages, then you may have been hacked, or there could be other technical problems, which need to be addressed. This is one case where more is not necessarily better. Google may think you have a bunch of duplicate pages on your site.

Here are just a few more ways to use the **site:** search operator to your benefit:

site:yourdomain.com -inurl:https

This search operator will help you audit your HTTP to HTTPS transition and discover any old HTTP pages that might not have been re-crawled by Google.

site:yourdomain.com intitle:car accident lawyer

This search operator will show you all of the pages on your site that are indexed and optimized for the keyword "car accident lawyer" within your title tag, revealing internal linking opportunities or cannibalization problems (which we'll explore in Chapter 7). You can replace "car accident lawyer" with any keyword of your choice.

Cache:

The **cache:** search operator will return the most recent cached version of a web page (provided the page is indexed, of course). This operator is different from the rest; instead of searching for it in Google like the others, you enter **cache:yourdomain.com** in your address bar and press submit. You need to be using Chrome or Google as the major search engine for it to work. This is a great way to see how often Google is crawling and indexing your content. We also use this search operator to confirm that pages with valuable links are cached and indexed. If not, we will use different pinging techniques to get Google to cache and index the page, so they see and follow the link passing both PageRank and TrustRank.

TrustRank is an algorithm that conducts link analysis to separate reputable webpages from spam. In other words, Google up-ranks websites that it trusts, and they measure that trust in their algorithm with TrustRank. The closer a site is to spam resources, the more likely it is to be spam as well. That is why it is important to be careful about which sites you link out to, and to monitor which sites are linking back to your website.

Find People Who Are Stealing Your Content

Copy a snippet of content from any page on your website. Then, take that snippet and conduct a Google search using quotation marks around the snippet. Follow that with **-site:yourdomain.com**. By using the **"snippet of text from your webpage" -site:yourdomain. com** search operator, Google will search for the exact phrase in your copy text and exclude any pages from your website in the search results. If Google doesn't return anything back, that is a good thing. However, if Google returns results with other law firms or websites that have the same exact content, you might have a duplicate-content problem that needs to be addressed.

Find Guest Post Link-Building Opportunities

Use the search operator as a link-building tool to find websites that accept guest-blog posts. Go to Google, enter any of these search queries into the search bar, and press enter. You will find thousands of link opportunities.

- "[your keyword]" + "write for us"
- "[your keyword]" + "write for me"
- "[your keyword]" + "become a contributor"
- "[your keyword]" + "guest post"
- "[your keyword]" + "contribute"
- "[your keyword]" + "submit a guest post"
- "[your keyword]" + "accepting guest posts"

If you are a criminal defense lawyer who specializes in DUI, you could use **"[dui laws]" + "write for us"** or **"[drinking and driving]" + "guest post"**.

Using search operators will help you refine your search queries, much more efficiently than using Google's normal search. Please keep in mind that we only touched on a few of the basic search operators, but their use can get much more advanced. If you are looking for all of the ways you can leverage advanced search operators, I highly recommend reading the book *Google Power Search*, written by a good friend and colleague of mine, Stephan Spencer. It's one of the books I keep at my desk at all times, and I reference it often when doing technical site audits or research projects.

People Also Ask

Another useful functionality of Google is its "People Also Ask" feature. By searching for a keyword or question, Google will most likely provide you with FAQs related to your initial search query. If you click the last question, then more questions will continue to populate. These questions can be an excellent source of content topics, as you build out your content strategy, which includes pillar pages and subtopics that speak to your audience's needs.

For example, if I type "Dallas car accident attorney" into Google's search bar, it might return the following questions:

- Should I contact an attorney for a car accident?
- How much is an attorney for a car accident?
- Should I hire an attorney for a fender bender?
- What is the average settlement for a minor car accident?

If you own a personal-injury law firm, these are questions that your target audience might be asking, and by creating a content strategy that provides answers to these questions, in the form of text, video, or both, you'll get more targeted traffic to your website and increase your chances of converting that visitor into a client.

PageSpeed Insights

Another free tool that can help you measure your website's performance is Google PageSpeed Insights. Simply type in your website's URL and click "analyze," then PageSpeed Insights will return a score from zero to one hundred for both the desktop and mobile versions of your site. It's important to note that these scores are different, and both should be taken seriously. All too often, people will only focus on their desktop page speed and not realize there's a different mobile score as well, and they'll wonder why their SEO strategy is not working. Think about this from Google's perspective: their client, a user, conducts a search, finds your page indexed, and clicks on it, only for it to take seventeen seconds to load. This creates a bad user experience for Google's client, which is why Google takes page speed so seriously. Bottom line: the faster and more reliable your webpage, the better chances you have of ranking higher on Google.

Not only will this tool give you a speed score, but it will also provide detailed technical suggestions for increasing your score and making that page faster. For example, the tool might suggest removing unnecessary scripts, compressing large images, fixing JavaScript problems, and a bunch of other technical jargon that you don't necessarily need to understand. The beautiful thing about this tool is that you, as a novice, only need to know how to put your URL in the tool and press enter. Then, you continue to do that until you score 90 percent or higher on both mobile and desktop. This is a great way to hold your technical SEO lead and web developer accountable. In fact, this is so important that I suggest you take a break from reading this book and go conduct this experiment now. Please note that if you have scripts running on your site, like Google Analytics, web chat, Facebook, or others, that will most likely lower your score.

Google Search Console

Google Search Console, another free tool, provides utilities and reports that measure your website's performance and identify technical problems. Google Search Console is in a league of its own, because it's the only platform that allows you to have a two-way conversation with Google. When Google identifies a problem with your website, you will be alerted and can take specific actions to fix the issues. There are so many benefits to this tool, but I'd be willing to bet that six out of ten people reading this book don't even know that it exists. This tool is how Google alerts you about manual actions and penalties; provides you with a means to file a reconsideration request if your site gets penalized; allows you to monitor, maintain, and troubleshoot your site's presence in Google's search results; and proactively or reactively guards against negative SEO attacks, by way of disavowing bad backlinks. We'll talk more about negative SEO in Chapter 13.

Like the other tools in this chapter, the insights gained from Search Console will give you a competitive advantage for ranking higher on Google if you proactively fix any and all technical blockers being reported. Without this tool, you are flying blind and left guessing why your SEO is not performing. So again, put down the book, grab some coffee, and text whoever is currently responsible for your digital marketing strategy, to make sure that you have this tool connected to your site.

Google Analytics

Google Analytics is another free tool that needs to be in your SEO toolbox. It is used to track website activity such as session duration, pages per session, bounce rate, tracking conversions and goals, among other things. Unlike Google Search Console, which provides leading indicators such as technical improvements that you can make to your website, Google Analytics provides you with lagging indicators of whether or not those improvements actually made a difference in terms of increased traffic, more time spent on your page, and your conversion percentages. In addition, because it's a Google tool, Analytics has direct access to search data and information from other Google products, that third-party tools lack.

THIRD-PARTY SEO TOOLS

As you can see, Google itself is one of the most powerful tools at your disposal. Google provides you with so many other free services, but there are plenty of valuable third-party software, and applications that fill in the gaps. Here's an overview of different tools that should absolutely be in your SEO arsenal.

Ahrefs

Ahrefs is a comprehensive, all-in-one SEO software suite that contains tools for link-building analysis, keyword research, rank tracking, site audits, and reverse engineering your competitors' SEO strategies. If I only had to pick a few paid tools that I highly recommend, Ahrefs would absolutely be one of them. In fact, I probably spend at least two hours per day using this tool.

What it does:

- Backlink analysis
- Keyword research
- Content gap analysis
- Technical site auditing
- Competitive analysis
- Rank tracking

Where to find it: **ahrefs.com**

Semrush

Like Ahrefs, Semrush is an all-in-one tool suite for improving online visibility and discovering digital marketing insights. They have an easy-to-use interface that can help you with your organic research, domain overview comparisons, link analysis, social media audits, pay-per-click tools, and even content marketing templates that will help you write and optimize your web copy to rank higher on Google. This is the other paid tool that is essential for your SEO and digital marketing success. In fact, if you polled a room full of SEO experts, I'd be willing to bet that nearly all of them use both Ahrefs and Semrush.

What it does:

- Runs a technical SEO audit of your site (or any other URL)
- Tracks your daily rankings
- Analyzes your competitors' SEO strategies
- Analyzes the backlink profile of any domain
- Provides relevant keyword ideas

Where to find it: **semrush.com**

Screaming Frog SEO Spider

Screaming Frog SEO Spider is a "spider tool" that crawls websites in the same way Google does. It identifies technical blockers and extracts data, for your SEO team to analyze and fix problems in real time. Unlike the tools mentioned above, Screaming Frog is a program that you download and run on your own computer.

What it does:

- Finds broken links
- Audits redirects
- Analyzes page titles and metadata
- Finds duplicate content and identifies canonicalization problems
- Generates XML sitemaps

Where to find it: **screamingfrog.co.uk**

Copyscape

Copyscape is a plagiarism checker that can detect duplicate content on the web. It both checks for plagiarism on your website, which is important if you're buying articles or other content from freelancers, and it checks for *your* content on other websites, so you can tell if anyone has stolen from you. Duplicate content can negatively affect your entire strategy, so it's important to deal with it quickly when it's found.

What it does:

- Checks your website for plagiarized content (you want to make sure writers aren't selling you duplicate content)
- Searches the web for stolen instances of your original content
- Sends you an email notification when it finds plagiarized content

Where to find it: **copyscape.com**

Siteliner

Siteliner is a service that scans your website and reveals internal duplicate content problems. Having multiple pages on your website with similar content can confuse Google and negatively affect your search rankings.

What it does:

- Identifies internal duplicate content
- Finds broken links
- Analyzes pages to reveal which are most prominent to search engines
- Provides reports on page optimization

Where to find it: **siteliner.com**

BrightLocal

BrightLocal is an integrated, local SEO and citation platform that offers cost-effective aggregator submissions and a citation-building service to help increase your local rankings. BrightLocal also offers tools for reputation and review management, local SEO audits, and an interactive dashboard with lots of useful data and metrics.

What it does:

- Tracks local rankings
- Audits and builds citations
- Local SEO reporting
- Multi-location tools and reporting
- Reputation and review management

Where to find it: **brightlocal.com**

Podium

Podium, a Google-backed venture, is a messaging platform that allows for easier communication with clients and leads. For example, you might use Podium to text clients, after their case concludes, and ask them to leave a review on your Google My Business listing or Yelp.

What it does:

- Manages reviews and allows you to communicate with customers online
- Makes it easy to send out standardized text messages
- Shows you competitive benchmarks for star rating, review count, and more

Where to find it: **podium.com**

UserWay

UserWay is an automated accessibility solution that will help make your website more compatible with the Americans with Disabilities Act (ADA) and Web Content Accessibility Guidelines (WCAG) requirements.

What it does:

- Enables user-triggered accessibility enhancements on your site
- Changes text size, font, contrast, and other formatting and design elements to be accessible
- Reads text aloud
- Moderates offensive content
- Reduces your liability to potential lawsuits

Where to find it: **userway.org**

THE SEO JOB REQUIRES THE RIGHT TOOLS

It might seem like a hassle to juggle so many different tools at once, but make no mistake: SEO tools are essential for success. A dentist wouldn't fix a cavity with their bare hands, and a contractor wouldn't build a house without a hammer. Just like that dentist and contractor, an SEO practitioner won't have much effect without their toolset.

Without insights and data, there's no way to know if your strategy is working, so you absolutely must track where you started, where your performance is now, and where you plan to go with your digital marketing goals to grow revenue and sign more cases.

SEO TOOLS

→ Google itself offers some of the most powerful tools in SEO: search operators, People Also Ask (frequently asked questions), PageSpeed Insights, Google Search Console, and Google Analytics.

→ Many third-party tools are available for link analysis, keyword research, conversion rate optimization (CRO), online visibility, technical SEO audits, internal and external duplicate-content problems, and every other area where you might need additional insight and guidance.

→ While there may be a lot to learn and manage, these tools play a critical role in the success of your digital marketing strategy.

CONTENT
STRATEGY

CHAPTER SEVEN

Content Strategy

Google is nothing if not a tool to search through the vast amounts of content created by other people. Without content, Google would not exist. It would be a single webpage with a search box and no results. This is why Google values content so highly, and why developing your content strategy is, perhaps, the most important part of your SEO efforts.

I've already talked about your high-level SEO game plan, but now it's time to dig deeper into the planning, development, and management of your content strategy. People often make the mistake of simply hiring a content writer, to churn out articles, without any guidance, structure, or information architecture. Even large companies that have been in business for years may be guilty of this approach.

For your content efforts to produce a meaningful increase in website traffic from your target audience, the content must be focused, positioned to outrank your competitors' content, tailored to your audience, and aligned with your overall SEO strategy.

WHAT IS CONTENT?

Before discussing strategy, I'd like to set the context by answering this question: what exactly is content?

Content comes in many shapes and forms, including text copy, infographics, and video. Here are a few ideas for content pages you might want on your website:

- Frequently asked questions (FAQs)
- Glossary of commonly used legal terms
- Penal codes in the locations you practice
- Information about your firm's practice areas and the types of cases you handle
- "About Us" page for your law firm
- Biographies for individual attorneys
- Contact information
- Client testimonials and case studies
- News, events, and press releases
- Scholarships and community involvement
- Career opportunities
- Engaging social media posts

- Blog (only if you're prepared to post regularly; a neglected blog reflects poorly on your firm)

These are just a few of the different content pages you'll likely want to include in your strategy. Content encompasses all the information that lives on your website, but for the purposes of this chapter and the strategy you'll create, I'll be speaking primarily about text on a page.

WHO IS YOUR AUDIENCE?

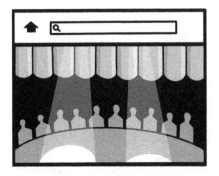

The first question you should ask yourself, in shaping your content strategy, is "who is our target audience?"

You want to attract more potential clients to your website, but who, specifically, will be the most profitable clients for your law firm? What is their demographic? What problem do they have? Why do they need a lawyer?

As part of this exploration process, you'll want to use the keyword research tools introduced in the last chapter, to identify terms and phrases your audience is searching for. You'll also want to turn to the research you've done in reverse engineering your competitors' content strategies. However, looking at your competitors is not enough on its own—aim to learn from their strategies, while staying within your own area of expertise.

By this I mean don't simply copy their content. For example, if a competitor specializes in brain-injury cases, whereas your law firm focuses on motor vehicle accidents, building out your content strategy around brain injuries is the wrong approach. Instead, make it your goal to take market share in the areas and audiences where you will excel based on your professional experience. Decide who your audience is, and build a content strategy that speaks to them.

WHERE IS YOUR AUDIENCE?

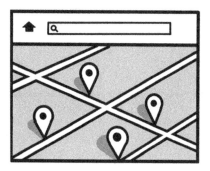

Once you've thought about *who* your audience is, you must cater to *where* they are.

The most effective way to reach your target audience is to create content specifically for your law firm's practice areas, and to tailor it to where your audience lives. If you're a DUI lawyer who serves (or wants to start serving) clients in Malibu, California, you need to create a webpage optimized for that geographic location. This guideline especially applies to areas where you don't have a physical location because you don't have the advantage of appearing on Google Maps. You need to insert yourself into that market, by having a targeted page optimized for that specific location and practice area.

When a user searches for "DUI lawyer" on Google, Google automatically knows where they're located and assumes they're looking for a lawyer in their area. That means if you don't have a page optimized for Malibu, a competitor who *does* have that geographic-specific page will outrank you in the search results and convert that to a lead.

If you're thinking, *This seems redundant. You're saying I need to create content for every small area in my market?* The answer is yes.

As people perform searches, for general phrases like "car accident" and "slip-and-fall injury," without typing a city name, Google tailors the search results to their location based upon their IP address. Again, if you're not listed on Google Maps for those locations, because you don't have a brick-and-mortar office, it is almost next to impossible to rank on Google for these terms. The only way to rank within those areas, short of having an office location in every market you wish to serve, is by having pages optimized specifically for those areas at the town or city level.

As an example, imagine you're a DUI lawyer based in Santa Clarita, California, but you also serve clients in Santa Monica, Burbank, and Los Angeles. You might want to have a webpage that uses a title tag optimized for "DUI Lawyer and Drunk Driving Defense in Santa Clarita, CA." On this page, the copy would express some sympathy about the potential client's situation, typically in the first two paragraphs, and include information about the penalties and consequences they are facing. You would also share information about how you can help and how they can contact you. You'd want to make this page hyper-relevant to Santa Clarita, by referencing the local courthouse and police department with external links to connect your webpage with the local municipalities. This is important because it allows Google to associate your webpage with authoritative and trusted resources, by way of a link and citation.

Next, you'd want to create similar pages for each geographic location you serve: "DUI Lawyer and Drunk Driving Defense in Santa Monica, CA," and "DUI Lawyer and Drunk Driving Defense in Burbank, CA." You would swap out the links for the courthouse and police department, to match their respective areas. However, here is an important caveat: *do not simply copy and paste content while replacing the city names.* This is known as "content spinning," and it stopped working as an effective SEO strategy years ago.

Each page must be unique. A page can express the same thoughts and advice, but the text on the page, the actual words, must not be copied and pasted. Otherwise, you risk your content being labeled as "duplicate content" by Google, which will hurt its search ranking. Google wants to see unique, high-quality content whenever possible. Yes, this really means writing a unique page for each of the cities you serve. It's a lot of work, but the firms that do this inevitably end up capturing far more leads than the firms that use a single, "one size fits all" page targeting the entire metro area. They put in the work, and they reap the benefits.

To optimize your website for Google's algorithm, you also want to avoid "cannibalizing" your own content. This occurs when you have two webpages optimized and, maybe ranking, for the same keyword. For example, you don't want different pages competing over the term "Santa Clarita DUI Lawyer"—the two pages will cannibalize each other, confuse Google and, in most cases, impede your rankings. Instead, incorporate as much content about this subject on one page as possible. By consolidating a subject onto a single page, the page will be more authoritative for that keyword and will provide additional information to satisfy the intent of that search query. This is why it's crucial to have a preplanned content strategy and trained copywriters, so you avoid these problems.

A word about coworking spaces and virtual offices: if you don't have a physical presence in a city, it may be tempting to pay a few hundred dollars per month to establish an address in a shared space, just to "be" in the city you're trying to target. Unfortunately, Google mostly disregards shared addresses where you can't prove that you have your own dedicated space that is permanently staffed by your own people. (And yes, Google will make you jump through many hoops to prove that your office is real.) This ends up being a waste of time for many law firms. If you don't have a physical presence in a target city, I recommend using the content strategy outlined above, rather than wasting money on a virtual space that Google will ignore and may even penalize.

CONTENT'S CUMULATIVE EFFECT

As you're creating these similar-but-unique pages for each geographic area in your market, a cumulative effect begins to take place. Every time you publish a page of content, Google crawls your website and indexes the new page. It triggers Google's algorithm to say, "This website is active and becoming more authoritative in a specific niche." It may even reward you with Google's freshness algorithm. The Google freshness update became part of the algorithm in 2011, and is based on Google's belief that content plays a bigger role in answering queries about current news topics than it does about dictionary definitions.

As you publish more content, each page, and every individual word on the page, populates in the form of a word cloud, algorithmically; then Google semantically associates the words and phrases together, while putting more emphasis and authority on the frequency and importance of the topics that you write about most. That is how the algorithm semantically associates you as a thought leader or trusted source with those who are seeking someone with your professional experience by way of a Google search, and how it makes the connection in under three seconds.

As you publish content that establishes you as a subject expert, your website's relevancy and authority grow. I recommend internally linking related webpages to one another, to associate and strengthen the web of content you're creating. For example, if you have a page that is optimized for the keyword "DUI Lawyer in Los Angeles," create side navigation, on the right or left side of the page, that links out to all of the other DUI pages optimized for other cities, using exact-match anchor text to link to their respective page.

Even though the links all exist on the same domain—what are referred to as "internal links"—they still add a *tremendous* value. If done correctly, they can make the difference in pushing these pages from page two of Google to the top three positions, where you will get more impressions, clicks, traffic, and leads. Internal links are one of the most underrated SEO techniques, which you can use to dominate your competition with Google.

Remember, Google's definition of popularity largely comes from the quantity and quality of links that are pointing to a given webpage. The greatest benefit of internal links is that they're entirely within your control. You have the power to audit your content, find relevant pages, and semantically associate them, by way of using internal links and keyword-rich anchor text. Your content builds on itself, cumulatively reinforcing the popularity and authority of each of your pages while passing PageRank and link equity.

THE SKYSCRAPER TECHNIQUE

When you Google a search term relevant to your law firm—"New York car accident lawyer," for example—look at the top results. How can you create a webpage better than the competition? What will make your webpage outrank the current leaders?

The answer, and a key tool in your content-strategy arsenal, is the Skyscraper Technique. The Skyscraper Technique, coined by Brian Dean, the founder of Backlinko, alludes to the following scenario: you're walking through New York City, surrounded by tall buildings, but have you ever walked by a *really* tall building and thought to yourself, "Wow, that's amazing. I wonder how big the eighth tallest building in the world is"? Of course not. It's human nature to be attracted to the best. And what you're doing here is finding the tallest skyscraper in your space, in the form of a webpage that is top-ranking on Google, and slapping twenty stories to the top of it. Now you have content that Google finds authoritative and that everyone wants to talk about and link to.

Let's say the top-ranking page for "New York car accident lawyer" has three thousand words of content. To follow the Skyscraper Technique, you might opt to create a page with five thousand words of content. The goal is to make something better and more comprehensive than what already exists. The Skyscraper Technique involves three easy steps:

1. Find a keyword you want to rank for on the first page of Google.
2. Analyze what content currently ranks in the top ten positions on Google.
3. Create content that's ten times better than what is already on the first page.

Once you've created your Skyscraper page, the next step is to reach out to websites linking to the competitor's page and ask them to link to your page instead. Convince them that your content is better—the taller, shinier skyscraper.

YOUR STEP-BY-STEP CONTENT STRATEGY

When we put all of the above advice together, what does this look like? Here is a high-level, step-by-step walkthrough of the content strategy process, some of which pulls from the work you did in previous chapters:

1. Identify your target audience.
2. Identify the markets you currently serve or want to serve.
3. Create a list of pillar pages and subtopics, generated from keyword research tools and Google's People Also Ask (related questions). Also, reverse engineer your competitors' websites for new content ideas.
4. Make a spreadsheet containing all the practice areas and geographic locations you want to target. For example, you might want to create pages about car accidents, slip-and-fall injuries, wrongful death, and social security disability. Plan to create a page for each of these practice areas in the

markets you serve: Santa Clarita, Malibu, Burbank, and Los Angeles. In this example, you would need to write sixteen unique pages (four practice areas for each of the four locations). From there, in the spreadsheet, create the URL structure, title tags, meta descriptions, and header tags that these page templates will follow. Also, give some consideration to how these pages will interlink and pass PageRank.

5. Leverage internal links to grow your website's authority and popularity, and to increase your search rankings.

6. Apply the Skyscraper Technique to make your page more authoritative and attract more inbound links, which will also increase your rankings, traffic, leads, and signed cases.

DON'T OVERCOMPLICATE CONTENT

A huge amount of legwork goes into planning and creating the high-quality webpages required to raise your authority with Google, but there's no need to overcomplicate the content process.

At the end of the day, your goal is threefold: become a subject-matter expert, have a presence in your target markets, and create better content than your competitors.

These are simple goals, but that said, don't underinvest in content either. Remember, Google *is* content, and the content on your website will make or break your search ranking. It's not enough to hire a content writer to publish blog posts without direction or focus—you need a targeted strategy that will position your website above your competitors.

Start with Your Law Firm's Core Area of Focus

You have dozens, hundreds, or even thousands of webpages to create. Understandably, this can feel overwhelming. You can't create all of your content simultaneously, so where do you start?

I recommend beginning with the practice areas that are most profitable for your firm. For example, if you're a Santa Clarita-based personal injury lawyer who primarily serves car accident victims, first write and publish a page optimized for Santa Clarita personal injury lawyer. Then, create a car accident pillar page optimized for Santa Clarita car accident lawyer. From there, continue to build out all of the other sub-practice areas for your Santa Clarita location.

Once you have these core pages published, now it's time to write content for your secondary market, tertiary market, and so forth. I would recommend that you take all of the cities that fit within a fifteen- to twenty-mile radius from your office, prioritize them based on population size, and match them to your top fifteen to twenty practice areas. This will give you anywhere from 225 to 400 pages of content to write, not including everything else, like FAQs, glossary pages, blog posts, and more. After you lay this foundation, it will be easy to gain market share by publishing new pages targeting other practice areas and geographic locations that stretch even further than the fifteen- to twenty-mile radius that you started with. Here's what this process might look like in practice, with example URLs.

First, create your top-level personal-injury page for your main geographic location:

- **www.yourlawfirm.com/santa-clarita-personal-injury-lawyer/**

Then build your sub-practice area pages for your main geographic location:

- **www.yourlawfirm.com/areas-we-serve/santa-clarita/birth-injury-lawyer/**
- **www.yourlawfirm.com/areas-we-serve/santa-clarita/car-accident-lawyer/**
- **www.yourlawfirm.com/areas-we-serve/santa-clarita/construction-accident-lawyer/**
- **www.yourlawfirm.com/areas-we-serve/santa-clarita/dog-bite-lawyer/**
- **www.yourlawfirm.com/areas-we-serve/santa-clarita/medical-malpractice-lawyer/**
- **www.yourlawfirm.com/areas-we-serve/santa-clarita/motorcycle-accident-lawyer/**
- **www.yourlawfirm.com/areas-we-serve/santa-clarita/nursing-home-abuse-lawyer/**
- **www.yourlawfirm.com/areas-we-serve/santa-clarita/product-liability-lawyer/**
- **www.yourlawfirm.com/areas-we-serve/santa-clarita/**

slip-and-fall-lawyer/

- www.yourlawfirm.com/areas-we-serve/santa-clarita/
  social-security-disability-lawyer/
- www.yourlawfirm.com/areas-we-serve/santa-clarita/
  workers-compensation-lawyer/
- www.yourlawfirm.com/areas-we-serve/santa-clarita/
  wrongful-death-lawyer/

Once you have sub-practice area pages for your main geographic location complete, move to your secondary, top-level, personal-injury location pages:

- www.yourlawfirm.com/beverly-hills-personal-injury-lawyer/
- www.yourlawfirm.com/burbank-personal-injury-lawyer/
- www.yourlawfirm.com/calabasas-personal-injury-lawyer/
- www.yourlawfirm.com/hollywood-personal-injury-lawyer/
- www.yourlawfirm.com/los-angeles-personal-injury-lawyer/
- www.yourlawfirm.com/malibu-personal-injury-lawyer/
- www.yourlawfirm.com/santa-monica-personal-injury-lawyer/
- www.yourlawfirm.com/studio-city-personal-injury-lawyer/
- www.yourlawfirm.com/
  woodland-hills-personal-injury-lawyer/

Then build sub-practice area pages for each geographic location:

- www.yourlawfirm.com/areas-we-serve/beverly-hills/
  birth-injury-lawyer/
- www.yourlawfirm.com/areas-we-serve/beverly-hills/
  car-accident-lawyer/
- www.yourlawfirm.com/areas-we-serve/beverly-hills/

construction-accident-lawyer/

- www.yourlawfirm.com/areas-we-serve/beverly-hills/
dog-bite-lawyer/
- www.yourlawfirm.com/areas-we-serve/beverly-hills/
medical-malpractice-lawyer/
- www.yourlawfirm.com/areas-we-serve/beverly-hills/
motorcycle-accident-lawyer/
- www.yourlawfirm.com/areas-we-serve/beverly-hills/
nursing-home-abuse-lawyer/
- www.yourlawfirm.com/areas-we-serve/beverly-hills/
product-liability-lawyer/
- www.yourlawfirm.com/areas-we-serve/beverly-hills/
slip-and-fall-lawyer/
- www.yourlawfirm.com/areas-we-serve/beverly-hills/
social-security-disability-lawyer/
- www.yourlawfirm.com/areas-we-serve/beverly-hills/
workers-compensation-lawyer/
- www.yourlawfirm.com/areas-we-serve/beverly-hills/
wrongful-death-lawyer/

Continue that process for each geographic location. Then, you can expand your content silos even further by going deeper with your content strategy. For example, if you were looking to expand your Los Angeles Nursing Home abuse silo, you could develop the following content strategy:

- www.yourlawfirm.com/areas-we-serve/los-angeles/
nursing-home-abuse-lawyer/bedsores/
- www.yourlawfirm.com/areas-we-serve/los-angeles/

nursing-home-abuse-lawyer/bone-fractures/
- www.yourlawfirm.com/areas-we-serve/los-angeles/
nursing-home-abuse-lawyer/bruises/
- www.yourlawfirm.com/areas-we-serve/los-angeles/
nursing-home-abuse-lawyer/choking/
- www.yourlawfirm.com/areas-we-serve/los-angeles/
nursing-home-abuse-lawyer/death/
- www.yourlawfirm.com/areas-we-serve/los-angeles/
nursing-home-abuse-lawyer/emotional-abuse/
- www.yourlawfirm.com/areas-we-serve/los-angeles/
nursing-home-abuse-lawyer/falls/
- www.yourlawfirm.com/areas-we-serve/los-angeles/
nursing-home-abuse-lawyer/financial-exploitation/
- www.yourlawfirm.com/areas-we-serve/los-angeles/
nursing-home-abuse-lawyer/malnutrition/
- www.yourlawfirm.com/areas-we-serve/los-angeles/
nursing-home-abuse-lawyer/wandering-and-elopement/
- www.yourlawfirm.com/areas-we-serve/los-angeles/
nursing-home-abuse-lawyer/sepsis/
- www.yourlawfirm.com/areas-we-serve/los-angeles/
nursing-home-abuse-lawyer/poor-hygiene/
- www.yourlawfirm.com/areas-we-serve/los-angeles/
nursing-home-abuse-lawyer/sexual-abuse/
- www.yourlawfirm.com/areas-we-serve/los-angeles/
nursing-home-abuse-lawyer/medication-errors/

While the exact URL structure is more of a personal preference, the goal remains the same: continue to expand your site, one page at a time, while developing the most trusted and authoritative resource for someone who may be doing research and in need of your services. The proven strategy, outlined above, will provide both the user and Google with what they are looking for, while strengthening your site with amazing content, all interlinking to each other, like Wikipedia does. This should exponentially compound your traffic, leads, and revenue, month over month.

There's no defined end to this content-creation process, because you can always extend your content branches, further, and cover more topics. The more content you create, the more opportunities you have to draw targeted traffic and prospects to your website. The key is to start close to home, with the bread and butter of your law firm, and then build out from there.

CONTENT STRATEGY

→ Content refers to everything on your website, including text, photos, videos, infographics, and more.

→ Google's algorithm places a huge amount of value on content. Without content, Google wouldn't exist.

→ To get results and boost your search rankings, you need to approach content creation with a strategy that prioritizes your audience, key areas of focus, and target markets.

→ Create localized pages for every geographic area where you practice. These can share a similar template and structure, but their content must be 100 percent unique, so they don't trigger any duplicate content filters or penalties.

→ Optimize single pages for specific keywords, phrases, and FAQs to avoid cannibalization problems.

→ Leverage the cumulative effect of content, by internally linking relevant pages to one another.

→ Apply the Skyscraper Technique, to overthrow the current top-ranking webpages of your competitors.

→ Start building webpages for your law firm's core practice areas, and then branch out from there.

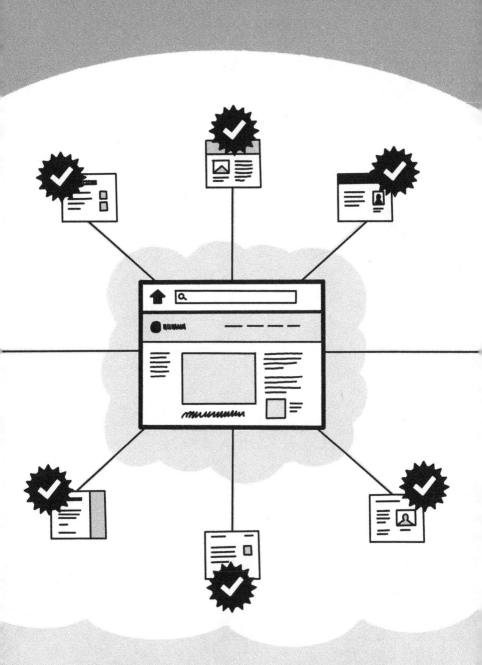

one link at a time.

CHAPTER EIGHT

Increasing Your Website's Popularity One Link at a Time

In Google's vast web, links are the strands that spiders follow from page to page. They bring people to your website, and they can either add to or detract from your credibility. In a way, they're the currency of the web, because if you have more high-quality links pointing to your website (called "backlinks") than your competitors do, your website has more value.

Links play a critical role in your website's ranking in terms of the three SEO components: relevancy, popularity, and integrity. As I covered in Chapter 3, you could have a technically perfect webpage, with well-crafted, relevant content, but without links adding to its popularity, that webpage could still linger in obscurity on the third page of search results. In short, your website needs links, and the popularity they bring, to secure high rankings within Google's algorithm.

SEEK OUT RELEVANT LINKS

When seeking opportunities for link building, you don't want any old website linking back to yours—you want to secure *relevant* links. Google is sophisticated enough to tell the context and subject of a website, by analyzing its keywords, links, and even images. In turn, Google assigns more value when relevant webpages become connected with one another. If a law school has a link on their website pointing to your law firm's website, the algorithm will consider it much more valuable than, say, a link from a bicycle shop pointing to your website. When relevant and reputable websites link to your website, some of the linking website's PageRank "flows over" and increases your own.

The same applies to relevant content, even if the linking website, as a whole, isn't relevant. For example, if a news site publishes a story about tort law and links to your law firm's website, Google understands that it's a relevant connection and rewards your site by boosting its popularity.

UNDERSTANDING YOUR LINKS

Links can help or hurt your website's search ranking depending on many factors: where the links come from, whether the links are reciprocal or one-way, how many links come from a single domain, the anchor text of the link, and more. Let's break down a few of the main things you should understand about links, so you can leverage link building to increase your Google rankings, lift traffic, get more leads, and sign more cases.

Referring Domains

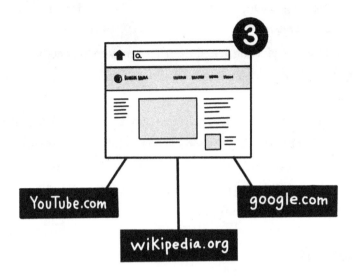

Many of the tools discussed in previous chapters will give you statistics on links, including the total number of backlinks pointing to your website, but in my experience, that's not the most important metric to consider. The more telling indicator of your link strength isn't the number of *links*, but rather the number of *referring domains* linking back to your website. Referring domains are websites from which the target webpage has one or more backlinks. Examples include: **wikipedia.com**, **youtube.com**, **google.com**. When analyzing your backlinks, if these three sites were linking to you, they would register as three unique referring domains.

Why is the number of referring domains more important than total backlinks?

Let's say one of your business colleagues has a personal website with five hundred pages indexed on Google. They put a link to your law firm's website in the footer of their website, and all of a sudden, when analyzing your link profile, you see the total number of back-links pointing to your website jump up by five hundred. *That's great for my site's popularity!* you think, but really, those links are coming from only one referring domain. Don't get me wrong; generally speaking, these links may have value, but not as much as you originally thought.

It's far more valuable to gain five hundred links, all originating from different referring domains, than five hundred links from one referring domain. In fact, having so many links from a single domain can negatively impact your popularity score if Google thinks you're trying to manipulate the system.

Anchor Text

Anchor text is the word, or words, attached to a link. Usually, anchor text appears underlined and in blue font. Google analyzes the anchor text of a link and surrounding text, when determining relevancy, so it's important to think carefully about the words or phrases you choose when adding hyperlinks (anchor text) within the body of your content. For example, if a blog post contains a link with the anchor text "Dallas car accident lawyer," Google connects the relevancy of those keywords, used in the anchor text of the link, and semantically associates it with the page that you're linking to. That anchor text provides context, whereas if the anchor text attached to the link read "click here," Google doesn't gain any useful information, and you're missing out on increasing the SEO of your website.

Google uses all this relevancy and context data surrounding links to combat spam. In the past, people would build links anywhere they could—usually in the comment sections of blogs—as a tactic to increase rankings. They would build a link using the anchor text "Dallas car accident lawyer," pointing back to their website, on a Coca-Cola blog post or forum, as a way to leverage Coca-Cola's popularity and authority while passing PageRank to their website. Today, Google recognizes that a car accident lawyer has no relevance to a soft-drink company, and may discount the value of that link algorithmically, or worse, if you're too egregious with these strategies, penalize your website.

Protecting Your Website from Link Attacks

One threat to be aware of, which I'll discuss in greater detail in Chapter 13, is an attack made by associating your site with toxic links. Competitors might actively attempt to sabotage your SEO efforts by building backlinks to your website on low-quality or spammy websites. For example, if a competitor posts a link to your website, on a site that has malware or spreads viruses to users' computers, being associated with that site will hurt your overall SEO. In the same way that high PageRank can help increase your Google rankings, being associated with sites with low PageRank could negatively affect you.

To protect yourself from these attacks, you'll want to have someone monitoring your website for unusual link activity as part of your regular, ongoing SEO efforts. The person monitoring your links should examine all of your backlinks and ask, "Does this link seem out of place? Could it be misconstrued as spam?"

Remember, both the website linking out and the anchor text should be relevant to your area of focus; otherwise the link's presence may look unnatural. With someone acting as your website's bodyguard, you'll be ready to fill out a disavow file—a way to tell Google, "I don't approve of this link"—which will disassociate the offending link from your website. You can determine the authority and respectability of a website by checking its Domain Rating with a third-party analysis tool like Ahrefs.

AVOIDING GOOGLE JAIL

If your website has been hacked or, worse, the SEO team you've hired has been engaging in black hat SEO practices or stealing content from other websites, you might end up in "Google jail" with what is called a "manual penalty." A manual penalty happens when Google's machine learning identifies a piece of content, link, or program on your website as spam. For example, maybe you forgot to update your WordPress plugins, and now there's a vulnerability on your website that steals site visitors' passwords.

When this happens, Google may register a manual penalty that tanks your search ranking and diminishes your traffic overnight. They will also flag all of your indexed content in the SERPs as suspicious, with a message that reads: "This site may be hacked." They do this for the protection of users conducting searches, to avoid spreading any viruses or malware. Fortunately, there's a way to undo the damage: Google Search Console.

Google Search Console is the only tool that allows you to have a two-way conversation with Google, so it's your only path for recourse. In Search Console, Google will bring the problem to your attention. Then, it's up to you to fix the problem and remove any vulnerabilities. That could be as simple as updating your plugins and removing malware, or as complicated as having to analyze thousands of links pointing back to your website as a victim of a negative SEO attack, then having to create a complex disavow file to submit to Google.

Once you've fixed the problem, you'll also need to submit what is called a reconsideration request. It could take a few hours to several days for Google to review your request and either remove the penalty or leave it in place. Until some-one reviews your case and removes the penalty, your website is stuck in Google jail. It is also worth noting that Google is vague in the way that they communicate these penalties. If you find yourself in this predicament, I highly recommend that you engage an SEO expert who has experience dealing with Google penalties.

LINK BUILDING TAKES REAL WORK

According to Google, if your law firm is a legitimate business, your website should gain links naturally. It will, but the attitude that your site can rank high with only passive link building isn't realistic. In order to be competitive, you must proactively pursue high-quality links, with specific strategies. Simply letting links happen naturally isn't enough. Where can you build these authoritative links that will help increase your rankings?

Here are a few ideas to gain high-quality backlinks:

- **LEGAL DIRECTORIES.** It might cost you a few hundred dollars for a listing in a reputable legal directory, but the link pointing back to your website may be worth every penny.
- **BETTER BUSINESS BUREAU.** The BBB is a trusted and highly respected website with a Domain Rating of 93 at the time of writing this book, which makes it one of the most valuable backlinks a law firm, or any business for that matter, could have.
- **SOCIAL MEDIA.** Your YouTube page and other social media profiles should each provide a link back to your website. With Domain Ratings usually in the high nineties (meaning Google recognizes the website's importance), links from these social channels can pass both PageRank and TrustRank depending on the attribute of the link. Be aware that while you don't want to duplicate content on your own website, it's fine to have the same videos on your YouTube and Vimeo channels, and other comparable platforms.
- **SCHOLARSHIPS.** By sponsoring a student scholarship, you can get backlinks from universities and other academic websites.

- **INTERVIEWS.** Have someone from an industry news website or blog interview you. The resulting article should contain a link pointing back to your website.
- **PODCASTS.** Whether you host your own podcast or are a guest, this is a great way to get more exposure and build authoritative links back to your website.
- **GOVERNMENT AND HIGHER EDUCATION.** If you can establish your website as a reliable information source or form a partnership with a government agency or university, you might be able to secure a .gov or .edu backlink. Google knows that not just anyone can publish on a government or higher education website; therefore, these sources make for exceptionally strong links.
- **PRESS RELEASES.** Put out a press release on topics like your involvement with a charity, the announcement of a new service, relocating your office, providing pro bono work, and more. If the release gets picked up by a media outlet, it will link to your website. Since most news sites curate old content, I would encourage you to write and syndicate a press release at least every three months.
- **JOB WEBSITES.** Post open job opportunities to websites like LinkedIn, Indeed, ZipRecruiter, Career Builder, Glassdoor, and Monster, and include a link back to your website from either your company profile or the individual job description.
- **REVIEW WEBSITES.** Make sure your law firm has a presence on websites like Yelp, and encourage your clients to post reviews.
- **BUSINESS DIRECTORIES.** Listing your law firm on websites like **yellowpages.com, botw.org, chamberofcommerce.com**, and **superpages.com** is an easy, quick, link-building win.

- **COMMUNITY MEDIA.** Another effective strategy for gaining backlinks is community involvement. Whether you do pro bono work, sponsor a local Little League team, or engage in some other kind of giving, your website will get linked to community webpages, local news sites, social media, and more.
- **COMPETITORS.** For more ideas on building backlinks, run your competitors' websites through a link-analysis tool like Ahrefs, Semrush, or Majestic. See which websites point to them, and try to gain the same links.

Not only will these backlinks directly result in more traffic from people clicking on them, but they'll indirectly boost traffic by increasing your website's popularity with higher search rankings. In turn, this will increase the number of leads and signed cases for your firm.

Publishing on External Blogs

As a subject-matter expert, it can be a win-win scenario for you to publish articles on other people's websites or blogs. They call this technique guest blogging. The site owner gets content, which will increase their traffic, and you get exposure and a backlink, which will increase your rankings and traffic. However, before you can start publishing, you need to find both relevant and authoritative sites that will accept and publish your articles. This requires manual outreach and relationship building. Don't be surprised if the owner of a site asks for a monetary administrative fee for their time to review and publish your article. In fact, some site owners might even offer to write an article, either for or about you, saving you time and money in content creation. Just make sure that you can review and approve the content before it gets published. In this case, this would be no different than paying a writer to write an article for you.

Now, you might have read that paying for a link goes against Google's quality guidelines, and while this "administrative fee" may be loosely interpreted as an exchange of money for a link, the reward is much greater than the risk, if executed correctly. After practicing SEO for over two decades, I can say with great certainty that, in order to rank high on Google for competitive keywords, especially in the legal niche, this technique is very effective. Don't get me wrong, this strategy is not easy and requires a lot of manual labor. However, the more effort you put in to identify and establish relationships with relevant blog owners who meet your minimum requirements, which we'll talk about shortly, your total number of referring domains will continue to grow, while increasing your rankings, traffic, leads, and signed cases.

If you work with a digital marketing agency, they probably already have relationships with bloggers who may accept your content. These bloggers might consider you a subject-matter expert and ask you to contribute one-off articles or even offer you your own feature column.

You might be wondering, *what metrics should I look at when analyzing and vetting guest-blog opportunities?* The metrics we use at Hennessey Digital for analyzing guest-blog-post opportunities include the following:

- Sites that are relevant to a specific niche or vertical
- Sites with a Domain Rating of 30 or greater, using Ahrefs
- Sites that rank on Google for at least one thousand keywords, based on Semrush's organic keyword trends

The best way to judge whether a guest-blog opportunity is worth an administrative fee is by making sure that the site in question meets these minimum metrics. Look at the site design and historical content published, and take into account your overall gut feeling, based on your communication and interactions with the owner of the site. If the site has a high Domain Rating, meaning it's popular and authoritative, is topically related, and meets all of the other requirements, the opportunity may justify the cost. Some webmasters might be happy to post your content in exchange for the future traffic that they will receive, while others may ask for an administrative fee ranging anywhere from fifteen to five hundred dollars, depending on many variables. Don't settle for their first price. I've seen administrative fees get reduced substantially just through negotiation.

Another approach is to reverse engineer your competitors' link profiles. You can even begin to reverse engineer strategies from law firms in bigger markets than yours. For instance, if you are a personal injury lawyer in a small market, conduct a Google search for a personal injury lawyer in Los Angeles, Orlando, or New York. Now, take the URL of their homepage and put it into Ahrefs, the link-analysis tool we've already discussed. From there, click on referring domains, and then sort their links by Domain Rating, highest to lowest. Finally, download all of the links onto a spreadsheet, and compare them to all of the links you have pointing back to your website, which creates a gap analysis for you to visually see the link patterns. If the highest-ranking law firms in the country have links from a particular site, it's a strong signal that Google is using these links when calculating the authority of their site in their algorithm, and it is probably why they are ranking so high on Google for competitive keywords.

OUT-LINK YOUR COMPETITORS

Always remember that your goal with SEO is to not only match the top players in your market, but to surpass them. Set goals for yourself to build a certain number of backlinks per month, and look for ways to gain a competitive advantage. Because Google search results are so localized, you're not competing with the entire world, only with the top firms in your market. Constantly ask yourself and your digital marketing team, "What will help our webpages rank higher than theirs?"

If the top-ranking law firm in your area has a link from a particular legal directory, you should have the same. You'll need to have as many or more high-quality backlinks to surpass the competition, and this takes real work. Furthermore, the work never ends. You can always find more opportunities for link building.

Whether it's writing content, recording videos, talking to interviewers, podcasting, submitting press releases, getting involved in the community, or simply submitting to be in directories, each of these activities takes time and effort to do right. You'll need someone writing content, someone doing email outreach, someone researching places to build links, someone handling social media, and more. Link building, like SEO as a whole, is a team effort.

As you can see, link building is not as simple as "the more links, the better." You must be scrupulous about which websites are associated with your own—inbound links and the anchor text used within the link should be relevant and from a trusted, authoritative source—otherwise you risk doing more harm than good. Take a slow and steady approach to link building, and over time, you'll see real growth in your website's traffic, while increasing your leads and signed cases.

WHAT LINKS DOES IT TAKE TO TOP RANK ON GOOGLE?

Over the past two decades, I have reverse engineered the link strategies being used to top rank on Google, for some of the most competitive and expensive legal keywords on the internet, keywords such as "mesothelioma lawyer," "cerebral palsy lawyer," "New York personal injury lawyer," and dozens of others.

Simply put, my team and I have invested hundreds of hours researching, analyzing, and studying the link patterns from over five thousand law firms, looking to see what the top-ranking websites all have in common in terms of their link profiles. Based on this data, I can confidently say that, if you can get links from the following domains, although not an easy task, while continuing to publish targeted and unique content on a monthly basis and maintaining the technical integrity of your website, you will take your SEO to the next level and start to dominate your market.

These websites are ranked by their Domain Rating, as specified by the SEO tool Ahrefs. The higher the number, the more a link from that website can help your own site.

Top Twenty-Five Legal Directories

Legal Directory (Domain Rating)

1. **lawyers.usnews.com (91)**
2. **lawyers.law.cornell.edu (91)**
3. **avvo.com (90)**
4. **findlaw.com (90)**
5. **justia.com (89)**
6. **superlawyers.com (88)**
7. **nolo.com (86)**
8. **martindale.com (85)**
9. **lawyers.com (81)**
10. **bestlawyers.com (80)**
11. **hg.org (79)**
12. **lawyers.oyez.org (78)**
13. **mediate.com (78)**
14. **thenationaltriallawyers.org (78)**
15. **lawyers.uslegal.com (77)**
16. **lawyer.com (75)**
17. **directory.justice.org (75)**
18. **lawinfo.com (74)**
19. **jurist.org (73)**
20. **wpattorney.org (71)**
21. **justgreatlawyers.com (70)**

22. **attorneyatlawmagazine.com (67)**

23. **lawserver.com (65)**

24. **getlegal.com (61)**

25. **enjuris.com (56)**

Top Fifty Foundational Links

Foundational Links (Domain Rating)

1. **facebook.com (100)**

2. **youtube.com (98)**

3. **linkedin.com (98)**

4. **pinterest.com (97)**

5. **en.wikipedia.org (95)**

6. **vimeo.com (95)**

7. **reddit.com (94)**

8. **creativecommons.org (94)**

9. **blogger.com (94)**

10. **yelp.com (94)**

11. **flickr.com (94)**

12. **bbb.org (93)**

13. **bing.com (93)**

14. **behance.net (93)**

15. **eventbrite.com (93)**

16. **medium.com (93)**

17. **sites.google.com (93)**

18. **yahoo.com (92)**

19. **business.site (91)**

20. **mapquest.com (91)**

21. **meetup.com (91)**

22. **prnewswire.com (91)**

23. wikihow.com (91)

24. businesswire.com (91)

25. about.me (90)

26. glassdoor.com (90)

27. indeed.com (90)

28. provenexpert.com (90)

29. prweb.com (90)

30. yellowpages.com (90)

31. crunchbase.com (89)

32. expertise.com (86)

33. scoop.it (86)

34. superpages.com (85)

35. visual.ly (85)

36. citysearch.com (84)

37. diigo.com (84)

38. prlog.org (84)

39. newswire.com (81)

40. chamberofcommerce.com (80)

41. company.com (80)

42. theodysseyonline.com (80)

43. topratedlocal.com (80)

44. dandb.com (79)

45. local.com (79)

46. muckrack.com (79)

47. dexknows.com (78)

48. ezlocal.com (78)

49. folkd.com (78)

50. botw.org (74)

Top 100 News and Media Links

News and Media Links (Domain Rating)

1. **news.microsoft.com (96)**
2. **forbes.com (93)**
3. **nytimes.com (93)**
4. **theguardian.com (93)**
5. **cnn.com (93)**
6. **bbc.com (92)**
7. **bloomberg.com (92)**
8. **businessinsider.com (92)**
9. **usatoday.com (92)**
10. **washingtonpost.com (92)**
11. **wsj.com (92)**
12. **abcnews.go.com (92)**
13. **npr.org (92)**
14. **cnbc.com (92)**
15. **reuters.com (92)**
16. **wired.com (92)**
17. **hbr.org (92)**
18. **fortune.com (92)**
19. **time.com (92)**
20. **huffpost.com (91)**
21. **cbsnews.com (91)**
22. **bizjournals.com (91)**
23. **buzzfeed.com (91)**
24. **dailymotion.com (91)**
25. **entrepreneur.com (91)**
26. **fastcompany.com (91)**

27. inc.com (91)

28. latimes.com (91)

29. marketwatch.com (91)

30. msn.com (91)

31. nbcnews.com (91)

32. theatlantic.com (91)

33. mashable.com (91)

34. usnews.com (91)

35. vice.com (91)

36. newyorker.com (91)

37. ft.com (91)

38. apnews.com (90)

38. bostonglobe.com (90)

40. cbslocal.com (90)

41. chicagotribune.com (90)

42. chron.com (90)

43. foxnews.com (90)

44. news.yahoo.com (90)

45. newsweek.com (90)

46. nymag.com (90)

47. nypost.com (90)

48. nydailynews.com (90)

49. people.com (90)

50. sfgate.com (90)

51. theconversation.com (90)

52. today.com (90)

53. vox.com (90)

54. patch.com (90)

55. rollingstone.com (90)

56. vogue.com (90)

57. boston.com (89)

58. seattletimes.com (89)

59. buzzfeednews.com (89)

60. vanityfair.com (89)

61. startribune.com (89)

62. cosmopolitan.com (89)

63. foxbusiness.com (89)

64. ap.org (88)

65. mercurynews.com (88)

66. nj.com (88)

67. msnbc.com (87)

68. dallasnews.com (87)

69. ajc.com (87)

70. denverpost.com (87)

71. ibtimes.com (87)

72. salon.com (87)

73. oregonlive.com (87)

74. sfchronicle.com (87)

75. baltimoresun.com (87)

76. insider.com (87)

77. esquire.com (87)

78. gq.com (87)

79. newsday.com (86)

80. cleveland.com (86)

81. rd.com (86)

82. sandiegouniontribune.com (86)

83. menshealth.com (86)

84. womenshealthmag.com (86)

85. mlive.com (85)

86. al.com (85)

87. detroitnews.com (85)

88. houstonchronicle.com (85)

89. ocregister.com (85)

90. orlandosentinel.com (85)

91. sacbee.com (85)

92. sun-sentinel.com (85)

93. washingtonexaminer.com (85)

94. money.com (84)

95. mic.com (84)

96. newrepublic.com (84)

97. reviewjournal.com (84)

98. laweekly.com (84)

99. natlawreview.com (83)

100. bloomberglaw.com (83)

Top 100 Educational (.edu) Links

Educational (.edu) Links (Domain Rating)

1. harvard.edu (92)

2. stanford.edu (92)

3. berkeley.edu (91)

4. princeton.edu (91)

5. cmu.edu (91)

6. columbia.edu (91)

7. psu.edu (91)

8. cornell.edu (91)

9. ucla.edu (91)

10. umich.edu (91)

11. **twin-cities.umn.edu (91)**

12. **upenn.edu (91)**

13. **washington.edu (91)**

14. **wisc.edu (91)**

15. **yale.edu (91)**

16. **duke.edu (90)**

17. **illinois.edu (90)**

18. **msu.edu (90)**

19. **nyu.edu (90)**

20. **purdue.edu (90)**

21. **ucdavis.edu (90)**

22. **uchicago.edu (90)**

23. **uci.edu (90)**

24. **ufl.edu (90)**

25. **ucsd.edu (90)**

26. **usc.edu (90)**

27. **utexas.edu (90)**

28. **osu.edu (90)**

29. **northwestern.edu (90)**

30. **rutgers.edu (90)**

31. **unc.edu (90)**

32. **tamu.edu (90)**

33. **arizona.edu (89)**

34. **ncsu.edu (89)**

35. **virginia.edu (89)**

36. **bu.edu (89)**

37. **indiana.edu (89)**

38. **gatech.edu (88)**

39. **georgetown.edu (88)**

40. iu.edu (88)

41. oregonstate.edu (88)

42. tufts.edu (88)

43. ucsf.edu (88)

44. colostate.edu (88)

45. cuny.edu (88)

46. hawaii.edu (88)

47. pitt.edu (88)

48. ucsb.edu (88)

49. unl.edu (88)

50. byu.edu (87)

51. caltech.edu (87)

52. rochester.edu (87)

53. uga.edu (87)

54. uiowa.edu (87)

55. umass.edu (87)

56. vanderbilt.edu (87)

57. gwu.edu (87)

58. wsu.edu (87)

59. dartmouth.edu (86)

60. ucsc.edu (86)

61. fsu.edu (86)

62. gmu.edu (86)

63. missouri.edu (86)

64. nd.edu (86)

65. uky.edu (86)

66. uoregon.edu (86)

67. usf.edu (86)

68. emory.edu (86)

Increasing Your Website's Popularity One Link at a Time

69. **ku.edu (86)**

70. **rice.edu (86)**

71. **uic.edu (86)**

72. **buffalo.edu (85)**

73. **miami.edu (85)**

74. **uconn.edu (85)**

75. **unm.edu (85)**

76. **northeastern.edu (85)**

77. **rit.edu (85)**

78. **temple.edu (85)**

79. **bc.edu (85)**

80. **utk.edu (85)**

81. **lsu.edu (84)**

82. **ucr.edu (84)**

83. **uh.edu (84)**

84. **case.edu (84)**

85. **drexel.edu (84)**

86. **fiu.edu (84)**

87. **sc.edu (84)**

88. **vcu.edu (84)**

89. **american.edu (83)**

90. **auburn.edu (83)**

91. **smu.edu (83)**

92. **umaryland.edu (83)**

93. **wvu.edu (83)**

94. **jhsph.edu (83)**

95. **ua.edu (83)**

96. **uab.edu (83)**

97. **baylor.edu (82)**

98. **calpoly.edu (81)**

99. **bucknell.edu (78)**

100. **syracuse.edu (78)**

Top Four Data Aggregators

Data Aggregators (Domain Rating)

1. **foursquare.com (92)**
2. **factual.com (75)**
3. **local-listings.data-axle.com (77)**
4. **neustarlocaleze.biz (73)**

You can submit your website to all four of these data aggregators, with any of the following paid services:

yext.com

brightlocal.com

moz.com

synup.com

advicelocal.com

LINK-BUILDING

🔍 TIPS AND TAKEAWAYS 🎤

→ Links contribute to your website's popularity and can either add to, or detract from, your credibility.

→ To increase your popularity, you need relevant links pointing to your website. Irrelevant websites linking to yours may look suspicious to Google and might create problems.

→ When analyzing your link-building activity, it's more important to look at how many referring domains point to your site, not how many links. You could have thousands of links coming from a single domain, and not only would it do little to boost your popularity, but it might actually lower it. A diverse selection of referring domains linking to your website conveys more authority.

→ Google analyzes the text surrounding a link, as well as the link text itself, called "anchor text," to determine a link's context and relevancy.

→ Competitors can maliciously attack your website by using negative SEO link strategies. Combat this by constantly monitoring your backlink profile, and submit a disavow file, when necessary, to disassociate your website with these potentially toxic links.

→ If Google suspects you of breaking its rules, your website might get a manual penalty. You'll then need to use Google Search Console to fix any problems and submit a reconsideration request.

→ Link building takes a huge amount of ongoing work and consistent effort. There's no end to the number of valuable links you can build through directories, social media, blogging, press releases, and more.

→ To successfully outrank your competitors in search results, you must have as many, or more, trusted and authoritative links as they do.

TECHNICAL

S E O

101

CHAPTER NINE

Technical SEO

By now, you have a solid understanding of how SEO impacts your website's search ranking. You're prepared to hire a digital marketing team, build a content strategy, and acquire the tools you need to achieve and measure success.

I've covered the basics, which leads us to the next step: the advanced concepts of technical SEO.

Technical SEO encompasses topics like URL structure and crawl errors—things that you don't need to understand in detail yourself, but should know enough about to recognize when there's a problem. If these issues carry on unnoticed, your Google rankings may suffer, or it may even prevent your website from getting indexed at all, so you want to quickly correct them when they occur.

My goal with this chapter is to arm you with enough information to hire a technical SEO specialist and hold them accountable. Too often, people expect their web developer, the person who builds the website, to understand technical SEO, but technical SEO requires a completely different skillset. I recommend interviewing the agency you hire and confirming that they have a specialist handling technical SEO audits, not a jack-of-all-trades. You want someone laser-focused on technical SEO; otherwise, nine out of ten technical problems on your website could easily go undiscovered.

Again, to find someone qualified and hold them accountable, there's no need to be a technical expert yourself. But it can help to know the basics. Imagine taking your car to the mechanic for an inspection. You don't need to know how to service your car yourself, but you should be aware that an oil change is part of routine maintenance. It's the same for technical SEO.

You should ideally have your specialist audit your website for technical problems weekly, or monthly at the least. If you work with a reputable SEO agency, they will likely have a technical SEO expert—or team of experts—who monitors for problems on your website daily.

TECHNICAL SEO PROBLEMS

What problems might show up on the technical side of your website? Among other issues, your technical SEO expert should monitor for:

- Crawl depth
- Cannibalizing pages
- Duplicated content
- Broken links
- Crawl errors
- Slow page speed
- Mobile accessibility
- URL structure

If you feel overwhelmed by the idea of technical problems, don't. I'll break down some of the issues listed above, but again, you only need to know enough to be aware that these problems may exist and to ensure that your hired professionals have them covered.

IDENTIFY PROBLEMS USING GOOGLE SEARCH CONSOLE

I've mentioned Google Search Console throughout the book, but I want to remind you of its importance in terms of technical SEO. Like a mechanic plugging a diagnostics tool into a car's onboard system, Google Search Console scans your website and identifies any problems.

It's your best tool for identifying technical issues with your website, whether they're accidental or caused by an attack or hack. The console also empowers you to have a two-way conversation with Google, so you can resolve your problems and get your website back in the search engine's good graces. It's like being able to whisper directly into Google's ear, and it doesn't cost a dime to use.

STEP-BY-STEP TECHNICAL AUDIT

To help you understand the role your technical SEO expert will play, in your overall digital strategy, let's take a step-by-step look at the questions they'll ask themselves as they audit your website.

Question #1: Is there more than one version of your website?

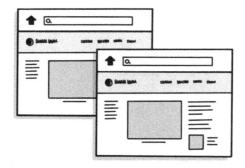

When Google indexes your website, it's important that it only looks at one canonical version. Typically, there are multiple variants that Google *could* be indexing, including but not limited to:

- **https://www.yourwebsite.com**
- **https://yourwebsite.com**
- **http://www.yourwebsite.com**
- **http://yourwebsite.com**

These are a few of the different ways a user might type your website into a browser—either with "www." or without, and either with the secure socket layer (SSL), "s" in "https," or without.

To avoid problems, you want to choose *one* of the variants and redirect all others to your chosen canonical version. I would recommend choosing one of the "HTTPS" secure URLs because security is a top priority for Google, and their goal is to make the internet safer, more broadly. On August 7, 2014, in a blogpost that can be found on Google's Search Central Blog, they even confirmed that HTTPS is a ranking signal in their algorithm, albeit a small one. Whether or not you choose to include "www." is a matter of preference. What's most important is to choose one URL and be consistent with its usage.

Question #2: Are there any crawl errors?

Next, your technical SEO expert will want to crawl your website, using a tool that helps you identify, audit, and improve common onsite SEO issues. I recommend one called Screaming Frog SEO Spider, which crawls your website in the same way Google would crawl it.

Screaming Frog SEO Spider will start at your homepage, and then follow every link located on every page of your website and in the source code. Depending on how big your website is, it could take as few as five minutes, or as many as five hours, to finish crawling every page and populating the data. When the tool is finished, it will show you the crawl depth of each page—this is how many links the tool had to follow from the homepage to the destination page. Most pages will have a depth of two or three. If you have pages buried as deep as sixteen or seventeen, you'll want to fix your internal linking structure to bring them closer to the homepage, also known as the root. This tool also allows you to analyze internal and external links, HTTP response codes, URL structure, page titles, meta descriptions, header tags, image file sizes, and canonical or pagination issues. Now, if this all sounds foreign to you, that's okay. This is why I recommend finding someone who knows what they're doing with regard to your technical SEO.

Question #3: Are any pages ranking for the same keyword?

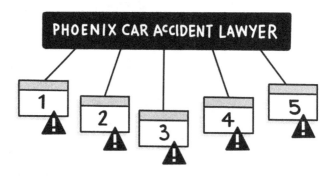

For every keyword or phrase relevant to your law firm, like "Phoenix car accident lawyer" and "Phoenix truck accident lawyer," you'll want to make sure there is only a single page optimized for this keyword and all of the semantically related keywords. For example, Google understands that "Phoenix car accident attorney" and "Phoenix car accident law firm" mean the same thing; while I would recommend including these different variations within the H2 and H3 tags (these are the smaller headlines you tend to see halfway down a webpage) and in the body copy of the "Phoenix car accident lawyer" page, for best-practice, on-page SEO, you wouldn't want to create unique pages for every single variation. In fact, it's just the opposite, and may hurt the effectiveness of your overall SEO strategy.

When you have more than one page optimized for similar keywords, these pages may cannibalize each other. Google gets confused —it doesn't know which page to index. As a result, both pages may never make it to the first page of Google, especially for competitive keywords. Google can get similarly confused if internal links between pages have conflicting or irrelevant anchor text. For example, you might have a link on a blog post with the anchor text "Phoenix injury lawyer" linking to your "Phoenix motorcycle accident lawyer" page and, while this may have been done unintentionally, perhaps even by one of your content writers, it can really confuse Google and hurt your rankings for both pages. Countless times, I've seen an untrained blogger writing and publishing multiple blog posts, all of which are optimized for the same keyword. When asked why they did this, they typically respond, "I thought if I had a lot of pages all optimized for that keyword, we would have more chances of ranking higher on Google for that term." I can't stress how damaging that may be to your overall SEO strategy.

Question #4: How can we improve PageSpeed?

The speed at which your website loads, known as PageSpeed, is one of the most underrated technical issues you can address, and it all ties back to one of Google's main goals: to provide a good user experience.

As former Google senior vice president Amit Singhal said, "When we slow our own users down, we see less engagement. Users love fast sites. A faster web is a good thing all around."

PageSpeed is critical to the success of your SEO campaign. According to 2018 research by Google, 53 percent of mobile users leave a site that takes longer than three seconds to load. This statistic tells you everything you need to know about why Google takes speed so seriously within their algorithm. It is highly unlikely that your site will rank on the first page of Google, for a competitive keyword, if it takes forever to load, because nothing kills a user's experience faster than a slow load time. In fact, if a page takes thirteen, seven, or even five seconds to load, many users will abandon your website entirely, rather than wait around for it to come through. Your goal should be to have your webpages load in two seconds or less.

Fortunately, Google developed a free diagnostic tool called PageSpeed Insights that provides you with a performance score ranging from 0–100 for both the mobile and desktop versions of your webpage. Please note that these are two different scores and should be analyzed and treated separately. To identify steps you can take to improve your PageSpeed on both mobile and desktop, simply open the tool, enter your URL, and hit analyze. You'll instantly get recommendations from Google on how to reduce your page-load time and increase your performance score with proactive measures like compressing images, minifying CSS, JavaScript, and HTML, improving server response time, eliminating unnecessary scripts, and setting up a content delivery network (CDN).

Question #5: Is the website mobile-friendly?

More people than ever before browse the internet on their phones or tablets, so if you ignore your website's mobile functionality, you're likely to give a large part of your audience a poor user experience. Because of mobile's popularity, Google rewards mobile-friendly sites and may punish ones that aren't. In fact, in a Google Search Console blog post published on March 5, 2020, Google announced that they would be switching to mobile-first indexing for all websites. What this means is that most crawling for a search will be done with their mobile smartphone user agent, prioritizing mobile experience over desktop experience when indexing content in the search engine results pages (SERPs).

Any skilled technical SEO analyst should ensure that your website loads properly on mobile, with these features: large-enough, readable text; accessible buttons and links; correct formatting and layout; and fast load times. To make the issue easy to resolve, Google offers their own free Mobile-Friendly Test, which can be found by searching for "mobile-friendly test" on Google.

Question #6: Are there any structured data errors?

"Structured data" refers to a standardized format, coded in the in-page markup, that classifies page content. For example, it's what tells Google that a recipe is a recipe. Recipe pages tend to all include the same elements: ingredients, cooking steps, time, temperature, nutritional information, etc. When Google recognizes, via the structured data, that a page contains a recipe, the page becomes eligible to appear as a graphical search result, which means it has a greater chance of showing up on the first page of Google with an image, reviews, ratings, and other Microdata.

Google's algorithm understands a page by looking at this structured data, so when errors are present, your page loses the boost of appearing as a graphical search result. In short, structured data errors rob you of quick SEO wins. To analyze and fix these issues, Google offers its own free Rich Results Test, which you can find by searching for "rich results test" on Google. In addition, everything you need to know about schema and structured markup for attorneys can be found at **schema.org/Attorney** (please note, you need to use a capital "A" in Attorney for this URL to work). I'd recommend that you have your SEO team or agency add this to your source code. Then, run the Rich Results Test to make sure that you are leveraging all of the applicable structured data options, and to confirm that everything was implemented correctly.

Question #7: Is there any duplicate content?

You know by now that Google hates duplicate content, whether it appears internally, on your own pages or, even more so, it appears externally on separate websites. This is why, as I discussed in Chapter 7, you never want to copy and paste content.

For example, you might need a page optimized for "Malibu DUI lawyer" and another page optimized for "Santa Clarita DUI lawyer," but they cannot be identical. Swapping out the city name is not enough to get around Google's grudge against duplicate content—the pages must be distinct and unique.

You might be thinking, *I wouldn't copy and paste paragraphs like that*, but two scenarios exist where you're likely to see duplicate content without knowing it. One, you might hire a content writer who, in an effort to save time, makes a template and simply fills in a few details for each different page. They might think this is a clever shortcut, without realizing the damage that it can create to your overall SEO strategy. Two, another website might plagiarize the content on your website and publish it as its own. In this scenario, assuming the guilty website is a law firm comparable to your own, Google should recognize that the content appeared on your website first, by the date it was published and cached, and then filter their content out of their index.

But what if an intern at a major news network, a website more trusted and authoritative than your own, decides to intentionally or unintentionally publish your original content? Google isn't perfect, and in this situation, it might rely too much on the authority and popularity of that website, ranking their page higher than your page in the SERPs.

No matter who steals your content, you'll want to take action and file what's called a Digital Millennium Copyright Act (DMCA) takedown. There's no reason to allow another website to steal your traffic and take credit for something you created.

On the other side of this scenario, your content writer, feeling extra lazy, might decide to intentionally plagiarize content from another law firm's website. You, as the owner of the firm, may not even know that this is happening, but if you're monitoring your analytics, a significant decrease in rankings and traffic will sound the 911 alarm very quickly. Google takes plagiarism seriously, and if caught using these tactics, your website will most likely be filtered from their index or, even worse, be given a manual penalty. For all of these reasons, it's critical to have someone monitoring your website and your content for internal and external duplicate content problems, using tools such as Copyscape and Siteliner. You'll want to address any duplicate content issues as quickly as they surface. There is even a service that monitors your site for plagiarism and proactively files DMCA takedowns on your behalf, for a monthly fee. This service can be found at **dmca.com**.

WHAT DON'T YOU KNOW?

With technical SEO, like every other subject, your knowledge falls into three categories: the things you know, the things you don't know, and the things you don't know you don't know.

This third category poses the greatest challenge because it includes subjects and potential problems that you aren't even aware exist. Many technical SEO issues likely fall into this category, and if problems like these go unnoticed, no matter how much money you are investing in your SEO each month, you probably will not see positive results or a return on your investment.

That's why it's so important to have someone who is proficient in technical SEO auditing analyzing and addressing these issues for you. You can't fix what you don't know exists, but you will sleep better at night knowing that someone who is knowledgeable in this specific skillset is proactively monitoring and addressing these types of technical issues for you.

ARMED WITH THE TECHNICAL SEO BASICS

The issues discussed above only scratch the surface of technical SEO, so I apologize that you have not become a technical SEO ninja by reading this chapter. But again, you don't need to be a technical SEO ninja. Armed with the basics, you can make better hiring decisions, understand the reports given to you, and hold the agency you've hired accountable, so you can see a meaningful increase in your site's rankings and traffic. My goal with this chapter is to educate and empower you with enough information to take more calculated risks when engaging or hiring a digital marketing team or agency, and to never be taken advantage of again.

As someone who has worked in this field for a long time, I've listened to so many stories where lawyers were spending thousands of dollars per month on SEO but weren't seeing any results. Self-admittedly, they didn't know what their agency was doing, nor did they understand why it wasn't working. In fact, most had hired and fired multiple agencies, over the years, who promised them the world but failed to deliver results. They were sick and tired of hearing excuses, over and over again, at their expense. Listening to these stories makes me cringe, because it gives all SEO practitioners a bad reputation. To be honest, this was my inspiration for writing this book. With the knowledge you have now, hopefully that cycle of disappointment can end.

TECHNICAL SEO

🔍 TIPS AND TAKEAWAYS 🎤

➜ "Technical SEO" refers to the functionality of your website: URL structure, crawl errors, PageSpeed, mobile readiness, and more.

➜ You don't need to become a technical SEO expert yourself, but you'll want to know enough to hold the specialist you hire accountable.

➜ Google Search Console is your most valuable tool in terms of technical SEO, because it identifies technical problems with your website and allows you to communicate with Google.

➜ Your technical SEO team or agency should be proactively monitoring, analyzing, and fixing your website whenever technical issues surface.

➜ By resolving any technical SEO issues you encounter, you can fine-tune your SEO strategy while gaining a competitive advantage in your market and increasing your rankings, traffic, and signed cases.

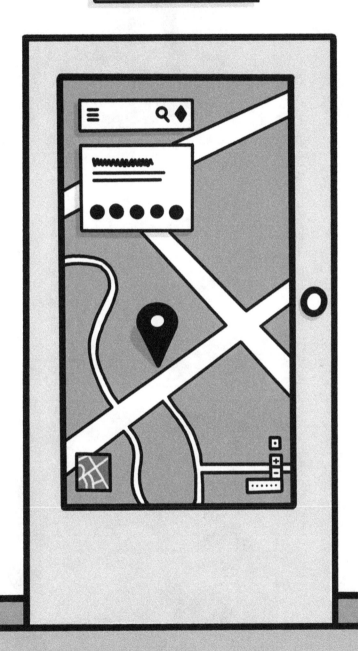

CHAPTER TEN

Getting onto Google Maps

When you're looking for a new pizza restaurant or hair salon, how do you find one?

If you're like most people, you probably pull up Google and type those keywords into the search box. In under a second, Google's algorithm uses location data and the three components of relevancy, popularity, and integrity to scan its index and create a customized list of search results. Then, the first thing you see on that results page, above every other link, is Google Maps.

Potential clients use this same process to find legal representation. They often reach out to lawyers in their immediate area first, which means if your law firm isn't listed on Google Maps, you could be missing out on their business.

CLAIM YOUR BUSINESS

Your first step to get onto Google Maps will be to claim your business. *Claim it? What am I claiming?* you might wonder.

You need to claim your law firm's business listing. Chances are that Google has already created a bare-bones page just waiting for you to come and fill it with more details. Start by going to **www.google.com/business** and creating a Google My Business account.

Google My Business is Google's local listing-management platform where you can edit your profile, list your business address and hours, manage and respond to customer reviews, add photos, and get access to your local analytics, among other things. You'll want to create an account and start managing your profile, as soon as possible because, right now, Google is relying on its data aggregators to pre-populate your business listing.

To claim your business, you need to prove you're actually the owner. This is to prevent a competitor or someone malicious from taking over your page and creating problems for you. For example, if someone listed a fake address or responded aggressively to reviews, it could considerably damage your professional reputation.

Google offers two ways to claim your business. One, you can opt for Google to call your business at its publicly listed phone number, at which point they'll call you with a confirmation code to verify your listing. You'll then need to enter the code into your Google My Business account. For the second method, which could take up to two weeks, Google will send a physical postcard to your law firm's location. Similar to the first method, the postcard will have a confirmation code that you need to enter into your account to verify your listing. Google may or may not give you a choice in which way you claim your business.

FILLING IN YOUR LISTING DETAILS

Once you've verified and gained access to your business's account, you can start to fill in the details and complete your profile. Your Google My Business listing includes the following:

- Description
- Photos
- Videos
- Address
- Website link
- Business category
- Contact information
- Questions and answers
- Client reviews

- Hours
- Social media profiles

Fill out as much as possible, and leverage every small tool Google gives you, because its algorithm values and rewards those who have completed profiles and are actively making updates. It wants to see you engaged with the process, so the more details you add, the better.

It's equally important to update your listing if any of your firm's details, like location or contact information, change. I've seen too many law firms lose potential business because they spent years with a defunct phone number in their local listing. Whenever something changes, you'll need to go into your Google My Business account and update the data manually. The algorithm, unfortunately, isn't sophisticated enough to reliably pull information from your site and keep your listing current, so updating should be part of your regular SEO maintenance.

NAP Must Match

The first details you should check and adjust, if necessary, are your law firm's name, address, and phone number, collectively known as NAP. If you take one piece of advice from this chapter, let it be this: *make sure the NAP on your Google My Business listing matches the NAP on your website.*

Wherever you have your firm's name, address, and phone number listed on your website, whether it's your contact page, footer, or anywhere else, it *must* be identical to the NAP on your Google My Business listing.

Your NAP details should be identical to what your bar license displays, and it should match with the Chamber of Commerce, the Better

Business Bureau, and other places it appears. Everywhere your law firm is mentioned, your NAP should be consistent across the whole worldwide web. If your law firm is called Joe Smith Law Firm, *that's* how it should be written everywhere, not "Joe Smith Law Firm" in some places and "Joe Smith, P.A." in other places.

Google's algorithm grows more intelligent by the day, but you still don't want to risk confusing it—or potential clients, for that matter—with inconsistent details. The more inconsistencies your listing has, the lower your chance of ranking high on Google Maps in that local area. The best practice is always to maintain consistency wherever your NAP gets published.

Add Local Schema to Your Website

After ensuring NAP consistency, your next step will be to add something called "local schema markup" to your website. Local schema markup is a type of structured data code (discussed in the previous chapter) added to your website that identifies local data when Google crawls your site. It's a way to communicate to the algorithm, "Here is verified information that belongs on our Google Maps page. This is our address, this is our phone number, etc." You can think of schema as a little tag that site visitors can't see, but Google's crawlers pick up on it in the source code and derive valuable information.

Hire a Google Trusted Photographer

Similar to Google Street View, which provides interactive panoramas from positions along many streets in the world, Google also has a program that will bring a trusted photographer inside your business to capture a 360-degree, panoramic virtual tour. Not only do the photographs look great and provide prospective clients a preview of your office, the virtual tour also gets connected to your Google My Business profile, and is one of the most trusted citations that you can get in terms of the Google local algorithm. To find a Google trusted photographer in your area, simply go to **google.com/streetview/business/trusted/** and search for someone near your office location.

Engage with Your Reviews

Reviews are one of the most important local ranking factors that contribute to whether or not you will show up in the maps for a localized keyword. Google has also gone to great lengths to weed out fake or paid reviews, and it values when businesses respond to customers.

For this reason, whenever your law firm receives a review, positive or negative, you should always try to respond to that review within forty-eight hours. If it's a positive review, thank the client for their business and for sharing their experience. If it's a negative review, don't get argumentative or go into detail about the problem. Remember, these reviews and your responses are publicly visible.

Instead, simply say that you're sorry they had this experience with you and you'd love to rectify the situation privately.

Google monitors and analyzes the reviews businesses receive, and the words and phrases people use play into the algorithm. It all contributes to the larger goal of defining the context and relevancy of your business. For example, if a client writes, "I enjoyed working with Attorney Frank Smith. He helped me get a great settlement after my motorcycle accident," Google learns from it. It sees keywords such as "attorney," "settlement," "motorcycle," and "accident," and adds each of these algorithmically, almost like a word cloud, to better understand the relevancy of your business and your local profile.

The more reviews on your listing, the more keywords, so always encourage past clients to add their perspective. Try to get a review from every single client. You can even semi-automate the process of soliciting reviews by using a service like Podium, which will contact clients after you've closed their case, via email or SMS. Often, all you need to do to get a review from someone is simply to ask.

Remember, reviews directly affect your local search ranking, so it's always helpful to be proactive and engage with clients. The content, keywords, and review rating all factor into where your law firm may appear in the Google Maps results and can be the difference between getting more phone calls and business, or being left wondering what is wrong.

Pay Attention to Insights

After you've filled out the details of your Google My Business listing, you can immediately begin to glean useful feedback from the platform's insights dashboard. This page will show you a wide array of details about how users interact with your listing, such as:

- What search queries lead people to your listing?
- Where are visitors located? Which zip codes?
- How many people have viewed your photos?
- How many people have clicked the link to get directions to your office?

When you review these insights, you can learn about users' behavior and adjust your listing and other content to better serve them. You might find that certain zip codes attract more potential clients than you realized, or your listing's activity increased when you added more photos. The point is the more data you have, the better.

MANAGING DIFFERENT OFFICE LOCATIONS

I've already discussed creating individual pillar pages for the different markets you serve, but there are a few more SEO actions you'll want to take if you own multiple office locations.

For each location, you'll want to create the following:

- Google My Business listing
- LinkedIn Page
- Better Business Bureau listing
- Chamber of Commerce listing
- Tracking phone number

I recommend using distinct tracking phone numbers for different office locations, which allows you to attribute incoming phone calls to their respective listing. Even if you have a single office or call center responding to every call, you can tell where the client is located based on which number they use.

Fortunately, you can maintain different tracking numbers without creating the NAP problems I described above. Google My Business gives you the option to list these tracking numbers for each location while still keeping your official business number consistent.

GOOGLE MY BUSINESS INFLUENCES YOUR OVERALL SEARCH RANKING

Let me ask you this: which law firm would Google list first?

A firm that has ignored its profile and only has outdated data pulled from other sources, or a firm that has full contact details, photos of their office, and engages with clients?

Knowing now how your Google My Business listing works, I'm sure you can see how the second firm goes much further in advancing Google's goal—to provide a good user experience—than the first ever will. That's why your Google My Business listing affects your website's overall search ranking.

The algorithm looks at everything: client reviews, photos (which I'll discuss in greater detail in the next chapter), how consistent your NAP profile is across the web, how many people have clicked "get directions to your office" from your Google My Business profile, and any other user behavior signals that Google monitors. Even without the SEO impact, having your contact and business details readily available is a powerful way to direct potential clients to your firm.

If, after optimizing your Google My Business profile, using all of the tactics we've discussed in this chapter, Google continues to populate the local results with lawyers who are closer to a given location, don't be discouraged. Sometimes, proximity will win out over the quality of the listing. Just like when you search for "pizza near me," there's such a thing as a lawyer being too far away. Google will only recommend your law firm to a certain radius of users, but by putting in the time and effort to make your listing robust and engaging, you can expand that distance as far as possible.

CAN I USE A VIRTUAL OFFICE FOR A GOOGLE MY BUSINESS LISTING?

The short answer to this question is yes; however, proceed with caution. I can count on one hundred hands how many times I have heard a lawyer who was using a virtual office complain that they were either not able to show up high on the Google Local Maps or, even worse, that their Google My Business listing got suspended. Some of these lawyers were legitimately working out of a virtual office, while others had set up dozens of virtual offices, in an attempt to game the system.

Per the Google My Business guidelines, "Listings on Google My Business can only be created for businesses that either have a physical location that customers can visit, or that travel to visit customers where they are. If your business rents a temporary, 'virtual' office at a different address from your primary business, don't create a page for that location. Businesses can't list a 'virtual' office unless that office is staffed during business hours by your business staff."

While this may seem nebulous, I can say with great certainty that a shared receptionist, who is not on your payroll, does not qualify as "your business staff." Don't get me wrong; I have seen law firms fly under the radar, for years, and get away with having a Regus or Davinci virtual office as their Google My Business profile. While there is nothing illegal about it, just know that if and when it does get suspended by Google, the damage may be irrevocable, and you could lose all of the time, money, and resources you put into optimizing that location; you may never see those positive reviews ever again.

Here are some other tips based on my professional experience:

- Do not use a P.O. Box as an address for your Google My Business (GMB) profile.
- Avoid using a shared, coworking, or virtual office, for all the reasons mentioned above.
- Never let another lawyer who practices the same type of law rent or lease a desk or room from you. If they set up a GMB listing using the same address and the same category as you in their profile, that is a recipe for disaster.
- Keep your name, address, and phone number (NAP) consistent on your website, your Google My Business Listing, and all online business profiles, citations, and legal directories.
- If you work from a home office, you can set up a service-area Business Profile, using your home address, but be sure to hide it in the settings. However, it is exceedingly difficult to rank in the local maps, for competitive legal keywords and phrases, using this method.

WHAT IF MY GOOGLE MY BUSINESS LISTING GETS SUSPENDED?

If your Google My Business listing does get suspended, don't panic. Sometimes making a slight adjustment to your profile will trigger a suspension, even if you are following Google's guidelines. My suggestion would be to find someone who has experience filing reinstatements, because these can be confusing and complex. Remember, time is money, and the longer your listing remains suspended, the longer your business and your bank account suffer. At Hennessey Digital, we have reinstated hundreds of these Google My Business listings over the years, and each case requires a unique strategy and incredibly detailed documentation.

In preparation for a Google suspension, which will most likely happen at some point, my suggestion would be to have the following documentation readily available. This will save you time and increase the speed at which your business listing gets reinstated.

- Set up a LinkedIn page for each office location.
- Have a Better Business Bureau (BBB) membership and profile for each office location.
- Take photos of permanent branded signage that may include your business name, on the outside of the building, on a street monument sign, within the tenant directory in the lobby, and on the inside entrance to your office or suite.
- Have photos of other images, as proof of your business's name and address, that may include letterhead, business cards, business license, city tax license, or documentation from your Secretary of State, for each office location.
- Have wide-angle photos of the interior of each of your office locations.
- Hire a Google Trusted Photographer to capture a 360-degree, panoramic virtual tour for each office location.
- Take lots of photos from your smartphone, with your GPS location settings enabled, and then post them to your Google My Business account for each office location. These coordinates are stored in the image file's EXIF (Exchangeable Image

Getting onto Google Maps

File Format) data and share location signals to Google.

- Create a seamless video of you, first, standing outside of your building. Pan the camera across any signage on the outside of the building with your name or the building number, and walk into the building while showing your business name on the building tenant directory in the lobby. Then, going up any stairs or on an elevator to your suite, pan the camera on your signage on the outside of your door. Move through your office where your receptionist greets you, while recording any other proof that you are located at this address (i.e., your business cards or letterhead with your address on it).

- Make sure that the address on the state bar matches the address of your main headquarters.

- Need more help? You can pose questions and even get answers from community experts at **https://support.google. com/business/**.

GOOGLE MAPS

🔍 **TIPS AND TAKEAWAYS** 🎤

→ Your first step to get onto Google Maps should be claiming your law firm's listing. It likely already exists with basic information.

→ Fill in as many details in your listing as possible: description, photos, videos, address, website link, business category, contact information, questions and answers, hours, and social media profiles.

→ Make sure your law firm's name, address, and phone number (NAP) are consistent on your website, Google My Business listing, and across the web wherever your business is listed.

→ Respond to both positive and negative reviews within forty-eight hours after clients leave them. Always be professional and helpful.

→ View insights from your Google My Business dashboard, so you can learn more about potential clients' behavior and proactively increase your rankings and phone calls.

→ Create separate pages for different geographic office locations.

→ Avoid using virtual offices, if possible.

→ Always be prepared for a Google My Business suspension with photos, supporting documentation, and even a video.

CHAPTER ELEVEN

The Importance of Photos and Videos in Your Strategy

Google's artificial intelligence can perform incredible feats, and one of the most impressive is the ability to analyze an image and recognize what it shows. The software, called Google Cloud Vision, can "look" at a picture and tell if it contains a person, guitar, dog, or any other recognizable subject. It can even read the emotions on a person's face and speculate whether the subject feels happy, sad, angry, or surprised.

Why does this matter for your SEO efforts?

If you understand how Google interprets your visual media, you can leverage photos and video to create a stronger association between your website and your chosen keywords.

HOW DOES GOOGLE SEE?

Google analyzes photos, using artificial intelligence, but we aren't talking *The Terminator* here. The program doesn't have glowing red eyes. So how does it "see"?

According to Google, Cloud Vision uses "powerful pre-trained machine learning models" to understand and interpret images. It assigns labels to pictures, based on millions of categories it has learned and defined before. Not only can the AI detect objects and faces, but it can also read text (both printed and handwritten), identify popular places and logos, and predict whether the content needs moderation.

Google's AI constantly grows better and more adept at identifying images. Every time you search for something on Google, you're helping it learn. For example, if you search for "guitar lessons," a list of search results will appear, and you'll probably click on one of the local business listings. There's a good chance that the company's logo might contain a guitar, or that reviews include photos of people holding guitars. When you clicked on the business, you told Google that the picture is relevant to "guitar lessons," and its understanding of what a guitar looks like grew a little stronger. It connected the keyword "guitar" with the image.

Once the AI has learned to recognize a guitar, the association goes both ways, and it can find photos of guitars, all across the web, and attach the "guitar" keyword to those websites.

LEVERAGING IMAGES ON YOUR WEBSITE

Google's association between images and keywords means that, by thoughtfully choosing the photos that appear on your webpages, you can choose which keywords get attached to your site. These images can live on webpages, in a photo gallery on your website, on your social media pages, or on your Google My Business listing, and the AI will associate relevant keywords with your domain.

For instance, if you post a photo of your business card, law school

The Importance of Photos and Videos in Your Strategy

diploma, or the front door of your office where your logo appears, Google's AI will read the text in the image: "law firm," "law office," "lawyers," "legal," and so on. Every visual word or subject the AI can identify will get associated with your website. It's worth it to include relevant photos on your webpages instead of leaving them text only, because of the visual SEO benefit.

Choosing the Right Images

You can now see the benefit of using images on your website, but how can you decide which photos to use?

My suggestion is to collect some photos you're thinking about using and go try Cloud Vision for yourself at **cloud.google.com/vision**. Using this tool, you can upload the image you're considering and see exactly which keywords Google associates with it.

Let's say you have two photos of damaged cars and you need to pick one to use on your car accident pillar page. You run both of them through Google Cloud Vision, and you see the keywords Google recognizes. For the first photo, the AI returns "car accident," "crash," "car," "bumper," and "vehicle." The second photo returns similar keywords, but not "car accident," "crash," or any other terms directly related to car accidents. Using this information, you might choose to use the first photo on your webpage because it will strengthen the page's association with "car accident" more than the second photo.

The idea is to strategically select images that will best optimize your webpages to rank higher on Google for your target keywords.

Gain Keywords through Image Labels

lawyers_office.jpg

Google's AI recognizes subjects in images, but you can help it along and add additional keywords to your site by strategically naming the files. For example, instead of calling your image files "image_1," "image_2," "image_3," and so on, optimize them with keywords, like "Phoenix car accident lawyer," "lawyers in office," or "law library." These optimization techniques provide additional context for Google to understand your content.

In addition to file names, you'll also want to add thoughtfully worded alt text (text read by screen readers and other accessibility

The Importance of Photos and Videos in Your Strategy

devices that describes an image for people with sight limitations) and captions (text that appears below or alongside an image to provide greater context).

Source High-Quality Photos

My next suggestion is to invest in high-quality images instead of relying on stock photos, especially if you're uploading them to Google My Business or other pages where they might be misconstrued as your own.

Google knows if an image is a stock photo originating from Shutterstock, Adobe, or any other stock source on the web. For this reason, I recommend taking your own photos, either by hiring a photographer (like the Google Trusted Photographers I described in the previous chapter) or simply using your smartphone. Take smartphone photos around your office, and you'll get the added benefit of having geo-coordinates attached to the images, which prove they came from your law firm's listed location. Remember, Google values authenticity, as a way to separate spammers from legitimate businesses. Taking your own photos tells Google, "We're a real business. Our address is what we say it is. This is what our office looks like." Sending Google this reassurance that your business is legitimate will, in turn, increase your rankings, traffic, leads, and signed cases.

Creating a Better User Experience

Gaining keywords from Google is half the reason you should make photos a part of your SEO strategy, but the other, equally important half is that images create a better user experience. People respond to visual information, and images break up chunks of text in a visually appealing way. This makes the text easier to navigate, and images—whether they're photos, graphs, charts, or diagrams—can supplement text to provide additional context and information.

One trend that can lower the user experience is for lawyers to put their faces all over their website. I say, "can lower," because using your face isn't always a bad idea. People respond emotionally to faces, and seeing a person on the webpage can build feelings of trust. But I would advise you to always make sure you satisfy the intent of the user first when deciding which images to include on a page. If a potential client searches for "car accident lawyer," think about what they want to see. What conveys the message, "We're here to help you get compensation for the injury you've suffered"? Overuse of your attorneys' faces can instead say, "This is all about us, not you," which is not the message you want to send.

As I've emphasized throughout the book, Google prioritizes great user experiences. If you can use visual imagery to enhance your design and provide a better user experience, the algorithm will reward you for it.

Images Can Drive Traffic to Your Website

Another benefit of website images is that they can drive traffic to your website. Imagine that you've hired a professional photographer to take photos of wrecked boats at a boatyard for your "boating accidents" page. Once those photos get uploaded to your website, if optimized correctly, they'll also appear in Google image search. If a user searches for "boat accident," they might see your photo and click on it, which would take them directly to your website. Another indirect benefit of these images is that people may link to the pages that contain them, which will pass PageRank and TrustRank, while also lifting your Google rankings.

LEVERAGING VIDEOS ON YOUR WEBSITE

Photos can be a powerful way to add additional keywords and signals to your website and enhance the user experience. Now, let's shift our focus to another visual medium: videos.

Videos, while similar in their benefits to photos, have a few unique strengths worth discussing:

- Videos can convey complex ideas and topics to visitors.
- Videos capture visitors' attention and keep them on the page longer.
- Videos are more entertaining and appealing than reading for many visitors.

Video's ability to keep site visitors on your page longer is especially important for SEO search ranking. Google's algorithm isn't listening to or watching videos; it's merely relying on signals to determine relevancy. Remember, Google gauges relevancy, in part, by measuring how long users view content after making a search query, before going back to Google and clicking on a different search result. As previously mentioned, they call this "pogo sticking." If a user stays on a page, instead of "pogo sticking" off of it, Google reasonably concludes that the content satisfied the user's intent for that particular search. It strengthens the connection between the webpage and any keywords contained in the search term.

Don't Embed Videos Using YouTube

A best practice you'll want to follow is not to use YouTube's embed links to add videos to your website. When you use a YouTube embed link, a site visitor will often interact with the video and click over to YouTube. Now, this visitor who you worked so hard to get to your website, using all of the SEO strategies and techniques discussed in this book, is on YouTube, watching music videos or the new trailer for *Star Wars* that everyone has been talking about. They didn't spend a lot of time on your page, which sends behavior signals to Google that your content may lack relevancy for that specific search query, and may negatively affect your search rankings.

The goal of videos is to convey information to users while keeping them on your page until they convert. For this reason, I recommend a video-hosting service called Wistia. Wistia lets you embed videos without linking to external sites like YouTube. That means when someone watches a video on your page, you have their full attention, which increases the chances of converting that visitor into a lead. Wistia also gives you detailed analytics about your videos, so you can see which videos are holding people's interest, where people tend to skip ahead in each video, and more.

That said, I still strongly encourage you to create a YouTube channel and post your videos there, as well. Second to only Google itself, YouTube is the second-largest search engine in the world. Millions of people use it every day; you definitely don't want to miss out on their viewership.

In fact, I recommend posting your videos to several video-hosting websites, because each platform is another potential link pointing back at your site. Not only are multiple video-hosting sites important to your link-building strategy, but they can also attract different viewers. Some users might frequent YouTube, while others watch videos on Vimeo. By covering all of your bases, you put your videos in front of more potential prospects.

Apply Video Schema Markup

If you recall, in the chapter on Google Maps, I discussed how local schema could be used to format your content in a way that fits Google's formatting standards. It allows Google to better understand the data contained in your content and increases your chances of ranking in the featured snippets.

Video schema markup works the same way. It's snippets of code you can add to your embedded videos, which assist the algorithm in understanding your content. Using schema, you can give Google the following information:

- Video title
- Description
- Thumbnail image
- Video length
- Transcript

Using video schema markup makes Google more likely to feature your video in the carousel of video results at the top of the first page, and it will increase your video's overall visibility.

Create Compelling Thumbnails

Many people choose books by their covers, and it's the same with videos. When publishing videos, you want to make sure to create or choose compelling thumbnails. When choosing videos to watch, people gravitate toward faces, so this is one area where using people in your images fits the best practice.

INVEST IN YOUR PHOTOS AND VIDEOS

A picture is worth a thousand words, and a video might be worth a million, and they should both be fundamental parts of your SEO strategy. Not only do photos and videos add valuable keywords and context to your website, but they also provide a better, more engaging user experience.

Creating high-quality videos and photos is an investment in your site that, while costly, may pay back dividends in increased traffic and, ultimately, more signed cases for your law firm.

PHOTO AND VIDEO

🔍 TIPS AND TAKEAWAYS 🎤

→ Google uses artificial intelligence (AI) to analyze photos and videos for keywords and relevancy, which it then semantically associates with your website.

→ Strategically choose images that will further optimize your webpages for your chosen keywords.

→ Take the extra time to optimize image file names, alt text, and captions with keywords.

→ Invest in high-quality photos that show your real office—Google values original, authentic content over generic stock images.

→ Breaking up your webpages, with images and videos, provides a better user experience and may convey information more clearly than text alone.

→ Videos keep visitors on your webpages for longer, which increases Google's relevancy score and your chances of converting that visitor into a lead.

→ Photo and video production can be expensive, but it's worth the investment because it may bring in new backlinks, increase your Google rankings, lift traffic, and generate more leads that turn into signed cases and revenue for your firm.

CHAPTER TWELVE

Turning Web Traffic into Cases

By following the strategies in this book, you'll dramatically boost the number of people who find and visit your law firm's website. But if those visitors don't actually become clients, what was the point of all your hard work?

To collect the return on your investment, you need to turn web traffic into signed cases. This is the moment when SEO meets offline work—when you make sure your office has an exceptional intake process to convince site visitors that you're the right law firm for them. From nurturing leads and collecting information, to scheduling a consultation and drafting an agreement, each step of your intake process brings you closer to a signed client.

SEO IS AN ONGOING INVESTMENT

Before I share strategies for converting website visitors into clients, I want to remind you—as I've mentioned throughout the book—that the SEO work on your website never truly ends. It's like the horizon, stretching on forever. You'll need to monitor and analyze your site's performance, produce new content, attract more links, continually optimize, and more. Don't forget that your SEO-savvy competitors are working on the same things, too. There's always work you can do to improve your website.

I don't say this to intimidate you, only to give you a realistic expectation of what it takes to have a high-performing website with Google.

The good news is that, after you start investing in SEO, your work compounds itself. The content you write today will continue to generate leads next month, and even five years from now. You make a large, upfront investment, when you build or redo your website and put the SEO fundamentals in place, and then it pays off over time. As your website's authority increases, your focus shifts toward growing your reach and maintaining your high search ranking rather than creating it from scratch. Over time, your cost per acquisition goes down as your current efforts build on previous ones.

Turning Web Traffic into Cases

SEO might seem expensive, when you're first starting, but I advise you to stick with it. Continue making the investment, and the cost-to-reward ratio will shift further in your favor the longer you keep at it. Your return on investment will continue to grow and compound exponentially over time as long as your SEO strategy continues to get implemented correctly.

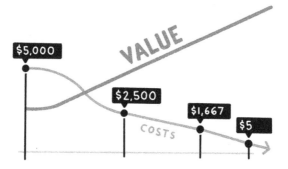

$5,000

VALUE

$2,500

$1,667

$5

COSTS

THE LONGER YOU INVEST IN SEO, THE BETTER

To see how your SEO efforts compound, imagine that you've spent $5,000 on SEO. From that initial investment, you generate five hundred website visitors. Out of those visitors, two people sign on as clients, meaning you spent $2,500 to acquire each client.

As you publish more content, your website's popularity grows, and having spent another $5,000 on SEO the next month, you attract one thousand new visitors, four of whom sign on as clients. Now that you've spent a total of $10,000 and signed six clients, this brings your cost per acquisition from $2,500 down to $1,667.

As you can see, the more targeted content you continue to publish and the more authoritative your website becomes in the eyes of Google, your cost per client acquisition continues to decrease. In a year, your cost per acquisition may only cost $500, because the content you published months ago is still generating traffic and bringing in leads. This is where the compounding effect really kicks in for law firms that continue to invest in SEO.

Turning Web Traffic into Cases

CONVERTING WEBSITE TRAFFIC

You can bring visitors to your website, but without a good user experience, they probably won't convert into clients. These people are looking for professional legal help and may have never engaged with or hired an attorney before; so your content, messaging, and user experience should convey appropriate empathy, trustworthiness, and competence.

Would You Hire Yourself?

Start by asking yourself, "Would I hire us? If I landed on this website, would I pick up the phone and call?"

Think about what you would want to see from a law firm if you had to hire a lawyer of your own. What questions would you have? What details, qualifications, or calls to action would you want to see?

Ideally, your messaging will include these points and entice visitors to take action. You've worked so hard implementing and investing in your SEO strategy. Now that you have a prospect visiting your website, don't leave such a crucial moment in the client journey to chance. I recommend personally reviewing your website's content on a quarterly basis. If the content on your website comes across as unwelcoming or confusing, for any reason, it might be time to retrain your copywriter.

Make Contact Effortless

Next, increase your chances of converting visitors by making it as easy as possible to contact your firm. A few best practices include:

- Display your phone number in the top right corner of every page.
- Code the page so the phone number remains visible, even when you scroll down. The visitor should never have to search for the phone number.
- Put a contact form on every page. It should be short, simple, and require only a single click to submit.

As the saying goes, a confused mind never buys. Make it easy for your prospect to connect with you by way of a phone call, simple form submission, or a web chat. By providing multiple options, you increase your chances of converting that prospect into a lead.

Show off Your Accolades

You never want to come off like you're bragging or flaunting a big ego, but if you've received accolades, show them! Potential clients feel stressed and vulnerable because they were wronged in some way, and they need to know they can trust you. Awards and recognition make a compelling argument.

Accolades you might want to display include, but aren't limited to:

- Association memberships
- Professional awards
- High **Avvo.com** rating
- Major verdicts or settlements

Again, visitors look for reasons to trust you—make it easy for them.

Don't Leave Potential Clients Hanging

Finally, it's the moment you've been waiting for: a potential client has picked up the phone and called your office. Now's the time to ask yourself, "Do we have a good system in place to handle calls?"

As a best practice, aim to answer calls within two rings. If a caller gets sent to voicemail, which hopefully they don't, return their call quickly, preferably within the hour. Don't leave them waiting. Respond to form-submission leads and web chats, preferably within an hour as well. I've seen and heard horror stories where a lead comes into a law firm, and because of internal inefficiencies, the lead is followed up with three to five days later. The chances of converting that lead into a client go down dramatically the longer you take to respond. Think about having a leak in your home; you call four plumbers, three of which go to voicemail, but you speak with one who can be there within an hour. Regardless of whether or not this plumber is more expensive, chances are you're probably going to hire them, simply because they answered the phone, were polite, and offered a solution to your problem.

At Hennessey Digital, we recently ran an experiment by contacting 732 of the top law firms in the country via their website forms. Amazingly, 33 percent of these firms took more than one hour to get back to us, and 24 percent of these firms took more than two hours to get back to us. To say these firms are throwing their money away is an understatement. At the same time, 54 percent of these firms contacted us in fewer than thirty minutes. Keep this in mind when you decide how important it is to get back to your potential clients

Turning Web Traffic into Cases

immediately. If 397 of the top law firms can get back to leads that quickly, what's keeping you from doing the same?

In the same way, you'll also want to create an effective intake script your office can use that demonstrates empathy and respect for a client's unique situation. This will help to prequalify all leads and move them closer to the signing process. You can get as sophisticated as you want with your system and even set up automated text messages to communicate and keep in touch with leads.

Using a call center can be a good option, as well. I recommend finding one that has experience answering calls for law firms. Their call center may answer after-hour and weekend calls for your firm, and some can prequalify leads, send hot transfers, or even sign cases for you. If you decide to go with a call center, my main piece of advice is to make sure you understand their process and are continuously proactive with the intake scripts that they follow. The last thing you want is to invest so much in SEO, in terms of time and money, only to lose a potential client forever because of one bad phone call.

A chat service can be a solid alternative or addition to hiring a call center. Available twenty-four hours a day, the chat service will essentially answer basic questions and collect a site visitor's information so you can follow up with them during business hours.

Make Your Website Accessible

Another important factor to consider for conversions is accessibility. Not only should your website be usable by everyone, so you don't turn away potential clients, but you're also legally bound, by the Americans with Disabilities Act (ADA), to provide accessible services. Many large companies have lost lawsuits costing millions of dollars because their websites weren't accessible to people who use screen readers, captions, or other accessibility features to interact with the internet.

To ensure that your site is and remains accessible, as I mentioned in Chapter 6, I recommend using a service called UserWay at **userway .org**. UserWay is an accessibility-compliance solution that helps ensure your website meets ADA requirements. The plugin will do things like enlarging text or reading content out loud, without you needing to hardcode changes into your website. It's a quick and easy way to make sure all visitors can access your content and services, and it decreases your liability for a potential lawsuit.

LEARN FROM ANALYTICS TO OPTIMIZE CONVERSIONS

At the end of the day, you can speculate about what you *think* is working, in terms of your SEO strategy and the return on investment, but why leave that to an educated guess? Let the empirical data help you make more concrete decisions with your strategy, to drive more traffic to your website, and then convert that traffic into more leads and revenue for your firm.

The data is available to you by looking at your website analytics. You want to know what drives conversions, which search queries produce the most leads, where potential clients are calling from, and more, so you can adjust your tactics accordingly. You might need to change your processes in one area, redesign a webpage in another, or double down on practice areas that net you the most leads or profit.

I've mentioned analytics throughout the book, but here are a few metrics that are particularly useful when studying conversions.

Call-Tracking Software

Most call-tracking software solutions have dashboards that allow you to track all of the calls that come into your law firm. You can listen to calls, see how long they lasted, track lead attribution, and even see the zip code where a call originated. Make the most of call tracking, by using dynamic number insertion (DNI) to assign attribution to inbound calls, using specific phone numbers that dynamically display on a webpage depending on the source of the visit to that page. For example, your visitors will see a different number depending on whether they came to your website via a Google organic page, pay-per-click campaign, Facebook, or any other traffic source.

Funnel Placement

Funnel placement means figuring out how invested or involved a potential client was before they converted into a client. Where were they in the funnel that goes from the general public to signed client?

For example, did they visit your website once and immediately call to set up a consultation? That means they were higher in the customer funnel. Or, did they visit your website several times, watch your videos, and read your whitepapers before calling? They were lower in the funnel.

Lastly, someone might have visited your website and left without contacting you. This person abandoned the funnel, and seeing where that happened can indicate that the webpage or piece of content needs to be more engaging.

Perform A/B Split Tests

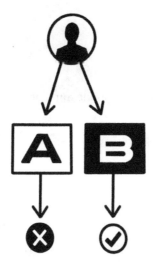

To take a sophisticated approach to compare different conversion-point options—like two versions of a contact form—try A/B split testing.

A/B split testing involves creating two versions of a webpage, one with option A and one with option B, and seeing which performs better. For example, you might find that over the same period of time, Contact Form A, which says, "request a free consultation," resulted in one hundred leads, while Contact Form B, which says, "request a consultation," resulted in only fifty leads. After performing this A/B split test, you now have quantifiable evidence that Contact Form A outperformed Contact Form B and lifted your conversion rate by 100 percent just by adding the word "free." Even if one option only boosts your conversion rate by 1 percent, over time, that difference can add up to an appreciable amount.

There's no end to the different site elements you might compare using an A/B split test, such as:

- Images
- Calls to action
- Button text
- Size and placement of phone number
- Forms
- Design options like fonts and colors
- Content
- Page titles

Running A/B split tests to see which conditions result in the most leads or signups is called conversion-rate optimization, also known as CRO. The more you engage in it, the better your site will be at compelling people to contact your law firm. Never assume that one design option will work better than another, because design is subjective—always test and validate your choices to get the best results possible. Let the data tell you what changes to make.

CONVERSIONS COMPLETE
THE SEO PROCESS

Gaining traffic through SEO is merely a path to the ultimate goal: signing more clients. The second half of that equation is to turn that traffic into leads by getting users to take action. You want them to pick up the phone, fill out a form submission, or engage in a web chat.

The best way to bring your SEO efforts to a profitable conclusion is to earn your site visitors' trust with a great user experience. Make it easy for them to contact you, and sympathize with them over the unique situation they're going through. Think about how stressful it is for someone on the other end of that phone to contact a law firm and ask for help with a personal matter. All too often, we get in the habit of answering dozens of calls every day, perhaps forgetting to take callers' circumstances into consideration. To avoid that, pay attention to every part of your intake process by listening to the phone calls, continuously optimizing your intake script, and training your intake team to be more efficient and effective when engaging with new prospects. What I'm trying to say is get inside your prospect's head. They are a human being with a family and real feelings, so show sympathy towards their situation, and be the kind of law firm you would want your mother to engage.

Lastly, remember once again that the SEO process never truly ends. For every potential client you convert, another two haven't visited your website yet, which is why you should continually strive to increase your traffic and reach. Rely on analytics and data to refine your processes and improve your website further. As your investment in SEO grows, so do the rewards. The more traffic you bring in, the more cases you'll sign and revenue you'll earn.

CONVERSION

🔍 **TIPS AND TAKEAWAYS** 🎤

➜ SEO will increase the traffic to your website, but it alone won't make people pick up the phone. Make it as easy as possible for potential clients to contact you, whether by email, phone, form, or web chat.

➜ Once people call, have a well-trained intake team that follows a proven script that is designed to treat your prospects with empathy and respect, while collecting the necessary information to see if you will accept their cases.

➜ Earn potential clients' trust by highlighting your accolades on your website.

➜ Don't neglect website accessibility—it could deprive prospective clients of fair access to services and create potential legal liabilities.

➜ Continually improve your conversion rate by learning from your data and analytics.

➜ Run A/B split tests to determine which of the two options performs better.

➜ Lastly, remember, SEO is a never-ending process, and the ultimate goal is to sign more cases and earn more revenue.

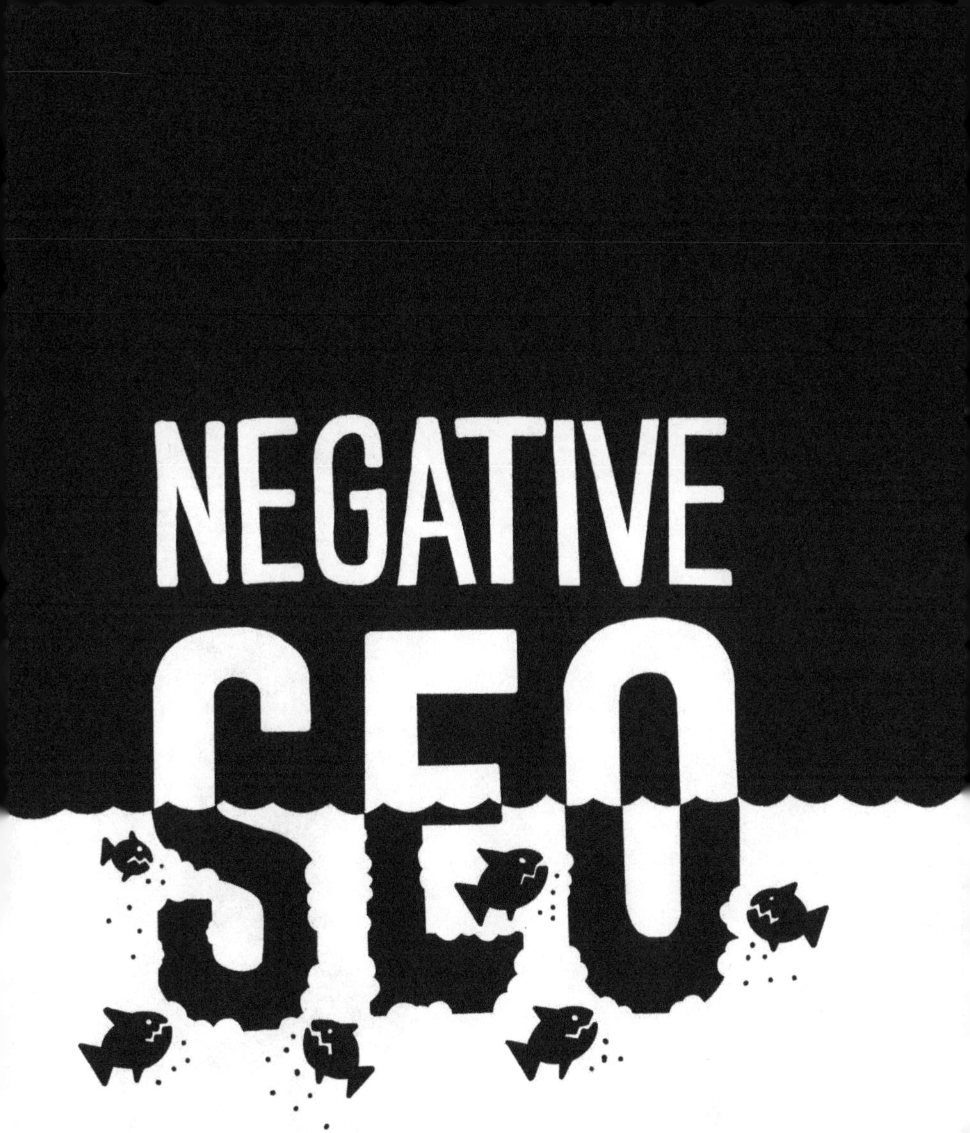
NEGATIVE
SEO

CHAPTER THIRTEEN

Negative SEO

You've made it—you've fought your way to the first page of Google, and your website traffic has never been higher. Now what?

This whole time, you've been playing offense as you tried to outperform and overtake your competitors' websites. But once you reach the top, it's time to switch to defense. You're the target now, and that means protecting your website from something called "negative SEO."

Negative SEO refers to black hat SEO practices and other malicious actions that people may use to sabotage your Google rankings. If someone malicious successfully pulls off their attack, your domain could even wind up in Google jail. As I discussed in Chapter 8, "Google jail" means your website has tripped an algorithmic filter—the result of duplicate content, spammy links, or other unwanted behavior—and received a manual penalty from Google. The consequences of receiving a manual penalty can be devastating, causing a decrease in rankings, organic search visibility, traffic, and revenue. Google gives out these manual actions as a way to protect users from viruses and vulnerabilities, among many other reasons.

Imagine that your website had been ranking on the first page of Google, but then someone with bad intentions managed to hack your website and inject a virus into your code. Now, whenever a user clicks a link on your website, the virus may attempt to extract their passwords and stored credit-card information. To prevent users from clicking your links and falling victim to the virus, Google essentially banishes your website to the later pages of search results, or may even remove you from the index completely. If nobody visits your site, nobody can get attacked.

However, this situation can wreak havoc for you because, without the proper monitoring systems in place, you might not even be aware anything has happened. A week or two later, maybe you'll realize you haven't been getting nearly as many leads as usual, but by then, the damage in lost business cannot be recovered.

YOUR NUMBER-ONE DEFENSE: GOOGLE SEARCH CONSOLE

Google Search Console has come up multiple times throughout the book, and for a good reason: it's your website's number-one defense system. Seriously, if you haven't already set up the console for your website, put the book down and go do it right now.

It's that important. Google Search Console is the only way for Google to communicate with you directly and let you know there's a problem. If you get a manual penalty, it will show up in the console. Unfortunately, Google doesn't always provide a great amount of detail, so you might need to do a bit of investigation to identify the issue.

Once you've figured out what's wrong, you'll need to fix the problem and file a reconsideration request. Depending on the nature of your problem, Google might ask you to document the actions you've taken to resolve the issue.

HOW DO NEGATIVE SEO ATTACKS HAPPEN?

If you're thinking, *I don't want an attack to happen to my website. How do I prevent this?* you have the right idea. Protecting your website means being proactive, because an attack can happen in several ways.

Spammy Backlinks

The most common negative SEO attack involves building spammy, toxic backlinks that point to your website. Usually, the attacker will unleash automation software that crawls the internet and builds links wherever it can—links to *your* website. Worse, sometimes the anchor text will contain pornographic or otherwise moderated content, which will raise red flags in Google's algorithm and get you in trouble.

Google doesn't know who's building the links, but it may assume that you, the website owner, are engaging in spammy behavior, and penalize your website. Your search ranking plummets, and if you aren't monitoring your rankings, links, and traffic, you might not even notice you're under attack.

If your website has a strong, natural link profile with links from trusted sources like *USA Today* and *The New York Times*, an influx of spam links won't instantly destroy your reputation with Google. Google takes your history into consideration, but you'll need to address the problem, quickly, by using Google's disavow tool to dis-associate your website from these toxic links.

The disavow file tells Google, "I didn't create these links, and I want nothing to do with them." Once you've disavowed, Google should block the association. It's like having a party with a security guard at the door, checking the guest list and only allowing those invited through the door.

Removing Good Links

Another attack, which is almost the reverse of the previous one, involves the perpetrator attempting to remove the good links you worked so hard to acquire. For example, they might reach out to the Better Business Bureau, while pretending to be you, and request that the site change or remove the link back to your website. Nine out of ten times, they will be unsuccessful, but those statistics won't stop them from trying. The only thing you can do is proactively monitor your new and lost backlinks, on a weekly or monthly basis, using a tool like Ahrefs.

Outdated Plugins

Another common way for negative SEO to happen is via outdated or poorly coded plugins, especially with websites built on WordPress. I cannot stress how important it is that you keep your plugins up-to-date if you have a WordPress site.

Because WordPress is an open-source platform, anyone can access the code, which means there are more opportunities for people to develop hacks and viruses. When this happens, developers push out updates to their plugins to close the vulnerability. If you don't update yours, your website remains open to attack, either by a competitor or an opportunist trying to take advantage of your situation.

If you have a WordPress site, I recommend manually updating your plugins whenever an update gets released. I suggest manual updates instead of automatic because, occasionally, a plugin update may break your website. For example, your contact form might be a plugin, and if an update breaks the code, you won't get any new contact submissions until you notice and fix the problem. When an update comes out, quickly look at the comments and reviews on the plugin's page, and if everything looks good, go ahead and update.

SEO Shortcuts

Negative SEO can also happen to your site because of ignorance and incompetence, more so than malice. For example, if you hire an inexperienced SEO individual or team, they might not even realize they shouldn't use automation tools to build links. They think they've found a great tool—until their client's website gets hit with a manual penalty.

Alternatively, they might be under the constraint of a tight budget and feel pressure to produce results. They decide to take shortcuts and use black hat SEO practices, with the hopes that they won't get caught. It might even work for a while, but Google is difficult to trick forever.

You can protect yourself from human vulnerability, by hiring a reputable SEO team or agency, and using the knowledge you've gained from this book to hold them accountable.

Distributed Denial of Service (DDoS) Attack

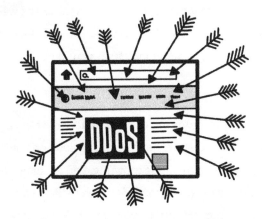

DDoS attacks frequently happen, even to larger websites, and involve flooding the target website's server with traffic. Most websites aren't set up to handle hundreds of thousands or a million visits an hour, so when their traffic hits a certain threshold, the server shuts down. While the server is down, visitors can't see or use the website. The longer your website is down, the more traffic and revenue you continue to lose to your competition, and the more suspicious you look in the eyes of Google.

Clone Websites

Yet another type of negative SEO attack involves a perpetrator making a clone of your website, with all the same content. Suddenly, all of the content on your website registers as duplicate content. With any luck, Google will recognize that your website has existed longer than the imposter and won't punish you. Other times, its algorithm doesn't recognize that the content belongs to you, and it will dock your rankings. In either situation, you'll need to file a Digital Millennium Copyright Act (DMCA) complaint to get the offending website taken down.

To protect your website from plagiarism attacks, I recommend using a service from **dmca.com** that will monitor the web for duplicate content and file a takedown request, on your behalf, if it finds someone is using your content without your permission.

Fake Reviews

You'll also want to monitor for fake reviews criticizing your law firm. Imagine that you have ten five-star reviews on your Google My Business listing, and then one morning, you wake up to find forty new reviews with only one star. This influx of bad reviews will crush your average rating and seriously hurt your Google local listing. If a fake-review attack happens to you, you'll need to work directly with Google, Yelp, or whichever review site was involved, to attempt to get the fake reviews removed.

Private Blog Network

Some digital marketing agencies use what's called a "private blog network" (PBN) to build links to your website, but this practice can get your website in hot water with Google if not executed carefully. A PBN is a network of websites, often owned by an individual or an agency. They use the PBN to generate backlinks for their clients and their own web properties, in an attempt to increase rankings and traffic.

While I've seen the more sophisticated SEOs leverage this strategy, with great success, those who are less sophisticated can kill the entire SEO strategy and cause a website to get penalized by Google. Google values authenticity. Its algorithm can pick up on patterns associated with PBNs, and when it realizes that you aren't building these links naturally, it may penalize your website.

To protect your firm, ask any agency you consider working with whether they use a PBN as part of their link-building strategy. Hopefully, they are honest and tell you "no," with reasoning. However, if they say "yes," proceed with caution. Don't get me wrong; I have many affiliate marketer friends who use PBNs to manipulate their Google rankings, while increasing revenue, but I wouldn't recommend using this strategy for your law firm. The risk is not worth the reward in the long term.

Click Fraud

One of the most expensive attacks that your law firm can suffer is called click fraud. In this attack, the perpetrator may use a bot, or human beings, to click on your ads, many times, using different proxies and IP addresses. This could easily cost you thousands of dollars in wasted budget, depending on the limits you set for your pay-per-click campaign. Google uses live reviewers, automatic filters, machine learning, and deep research to block as much invalid and fraudulent activity as possible, but you should actively monitor your campaign and report anything suspicious to Google.

Gaining Access to Your Site

If someone malicious gains access to your website's code, they can cause a ton of damage. For example, they might de-index your website with Google, meaning your website won't show up in search results at all. Remember, when you see search results, you're looking at a snapshot of Google's index, not a live, real-time scan of the internet. When this happens, unless you know precisely what to look for in the source code, it can be difficult to identify and fix the problem.

How might someone gain access to your website?

A disgruntled former employee who still has access to your server could go in and break things. If you have weak security measures and passwords, someone could hack into your site. Or, if you don't have administrative privileges, an agency or hired professional could hypothetically take control and hold your website hostage.

To protect your website from unwanted access, you need protocols in place for handling security. Best practices include things like:

- **USING SECURE PASSWORDS.** A secure password should contain a combination of upper and lowercase letters, numbers, and symbols. It can be made even more secure by avoiding the inclusion of any recognizable words or names. Whatever you do, make sure that you don't reuse the same passwords on a bunch of sites. I recommend using a password manager, such as LastPass or 1Password, to make it easy to use unique passwords that are nearly impossible for hackers to guess.

- **RETAINING ADMINISTRATOR PRIVILEGES YOURSELF.** If you have to burn bridges with an agency or professional for some reason, the last thing you want is for your website to be solely in their hands. You should have administrative privileges to both your website and your server, so you can revoke others' access if needed.

- **HAVING A SYSTEM TO HANDLE EMPLOYEE ACCESS.** Along the same lines as the first two practices, you want a system in place for handling security whenever an employee leaves or joins the company. If an employee gets fired, you'll want to revoke their website access immediately. Even if an employee leaves on good terms, don't leave their access open. You have no idea what they might do a few years down the line, and there's no reason to risk your website's security. I recommend using a service like **okta.com**, which provides secure identity management with a single sign-on, making it easier when someone leaves your firm.

Your website's security is of the highest importance, so make sure the agency you hire has protocols in place to protect it from hackers, vulnerabilities, and malware. Also, make sure that your hosting company has both automated and manual backups to help protect your data, which can be restored, in minutes, if your website is compromised. Trust me; you will sleep better at night.

ARE NEGATIVE SEO ATTACKS BECOMING MORE COMMON?

You might be wondering, how common are these attacks? How likely is it that they'll happen to me?

While negative SEO is not a very common practice, as your website grows, in terms of authority and popularity, you become a bigger target for these types of attacks. If you're just starting out, your website likely doesn't pose enough threat or temptation to be much of a target. However, as your PageRank and TrustRank continue to grow, and you begin to rank high on Google for competitive terms, you become more vulnerable to this type of attack.

In most cases, it's not your direct competitors who are engaging in these types of unethical practices. We see negative SEO more from anonymous lead-generation companies, spammers, or those working on behalf of a law firm, where the law-firm owner is not aware that these shady tactics are being used. Remember, your SEO success is very transparent to others, who may be jealous or vindictive, and they may have no problem using unscrupulous practices to compete.

Unfortunately, there's not much incentive for people to abstain from committing these attacks. By using a tool called a virtual private network (VPN), attackers can obscure their location, which makes it incredibly difficult to determine who is behind an attack. From what I've seen throughout my career, there's approximately a 98 percent chance you'll never catch the person who did it.

Another confounding factor is the tech-savviness of young people today. Every few months you hear a news story about yet another teenager who's managed to hack a celebrity's Twitter account or a company's website. Web attacks in general are increasing in frequency, partly because it's easier than ever to learn how to perpetrate them. With an abundance of free coding resources and a computer in nearly every home in America, the opportunity for mischief is there, for anyone willing to take it. People can change the world for the better with computers, but they can also do a lot of evil.

Negative SEO attacks aren't going away anytime soon, so as a law-firm owner, it pays to be prepared and proactive when it comes to your web security and protecting your investment. Establish good practices now, because as the saying goes, "An ounce of prevention is worth a pound of cure."

NEGATIVE SEO

🔍 TIPS AND TAKEAWAYS 🎤

→ Reaching the first page of Google means switching from offense to defense. Now you must defend your rankings and protect your website from potential attacks.

→ Google Search Console is your best defense against negative SEO. The console helps to provide insights, when your website has a problem, so you can take quick action to resolve it.

→ Malicious individuals may attack your website in all manner of ways: spammy backlinks, removing good links, outdated plugin vulnerabilities, black hat SEO techniques, distributed denial of service attack, cloned websites, fake reviews, private blog networks, and click fraud.

→ Negative SEO attacks will only become more of a problem as young, technologically savvy people grow up with access to free educational resources that teach them these unethical practices.

→ Proactively monitor your website for attacks, and take preventative steps to protect your SEO investment.

Conclusion

I've covered a lot of ground in the last thirteen chapters, and by now you've probably realized SEO is a deeper, more involved field than you expected before opening this book. But I want to repeat something I said at the beginning: don't feel overwhelmed.

You're armed with the SEO basics and have the knowledge you need to take action. I recommend going back to Chapter 1 and skimming through the book again, while creating a detailed action plan that you and your team can follow. In fact, I hope you keep this book at your desk and reference it frequently as you carry out and manage those in charge of your SEO strategy. You'll pick up on details you missed the first time and more clearly see how different SEO practices fit together.

ACTION CREATES RESULTS

boils down to the two ways you can get more traffic: boosting your popularity, with link building; and becoming an authoritative source, by writing and publishing more targeted content. These two activities deserve the most attention, and they also require the most ongoing work. However, together they will only be effective as long as you continuously monitor, fix, and keep up with technical SEO best practices. As you learn more, from experience and analytics, you'll want to monitor your rankings, reoptimize pages, and strengthen content as necessary.

Growth won't happen overnight—SEO is a never-ending process of continual monitoring, maintenance, and improvement. You can't check a box and be done with it. On the contrary, you could have an agency of one hundred people working on your website, and they would still find improvements to make. There's always more content to write, more links to build, more conversion factors to optimize, and more analysis to perform. The work never ends, so I encourage you to have patience and celebrate the little wins. Each step forward means more potential clients picking up the phone to call you.

TAKE ON THE COMPETITION

You're starting at the ground level, and right now, you need to lay the foundation. Today, your website might appear on page fourteen of Google, but keep at it—you're playing a competitive game of inches. Before long, your site will be on page eleven, then page seven, then four, until one day, you'll see it at the top.

Don't be discouraged by the time it takes because, remember, you may be competing against law firms that have been working at this for years. Give yourself time to catch up. I know that, as a lawyer, you aren't afraid of competition. You probably thrive on it. Good. Success in SEO is all about studying the competition, reverse engineering their strategy, and then beating them at their own game.

Throughout the process, keep in mind that Google's algorithm is constantly in flux. You'll see setbacks and shifts where your website moves up and down in the search results. This "Google dance," also known as Everflux, happens to all websites and is nothing to worry about. It certainly doesn't mean you've lost. As long as you consistently provide an excellent user experience, create high-quality content, and manage your website's integrity, your site will be seen as a trusted source of information to Google.

INVEST IN YOUR WEBSITE'S SUCCESS

Whether you build a team in-house or hire an agency is up to you, but in my experience, you'll see better, faster results by working with a full team of experienced professionals. Either way, it's your job to understand what your team is doing and hold them accountable. With the knowledge you possess now, the days of self-proclaimed experts being able to take advantage of you are over. You can and will make your investment in SEO a good one.

The cost of hiring an agency might seem steep upfront, but skilled SEO work compounds and pays dividends. How many dividends?

That question brings to mind a story about a client who went all-in on his investment in SEO. Determined to make his law firm rank number one in his market, we got to work. Every month, our team wrote about a hundred thousand words of content and worked with a large SEO budget. Eight months later I visited my client in his office, because he planned to go out to dinner with the team.

I found him at his desk, face red, with a bottle of blood pressure pills and a stack of paperwork in front of him. "I can't go out with you guys tonight," he said. "I have too much work."

Our SEO efforts had been so successful that the firm now had too many signed cases to handle. He was going to have to spend all night in the office, filing papers and preparing cases. He looked at me and said, "Is there any way we could just slow down the SEO for a month until I can find more people to hire?"

But I had to tell him no, SEO is like a broken fire hydrant, there's no turning it off. Fortunately, within a week, my client had hired more employees—the surge in cases meant he had the revenue to quickly grow his team. Since then, his law firm has been more successful than ever.

Done well, SEO is the rocket fuel that helps you launch. It's the fertilizer that turns your grass green. Follow the advice in this book, and execute your strategy right, and SEO will help you sign so many cases that you'll have to hire more attorneys to keep up with demand.

I hope you close this book feeling confident and capable of taking on SEO. If you'd like to learn more about working with our digital marketing team, please visit us at **hennessey.com**. *Mention this book, and we'll be more than happy to give you a complimentary website audit to get you started on your SEO journey.*

Acknowledgments

The first person whom I want to acknowledge is my mother, JoAnn, who had me at eighteen years old, and sacrificed everything to raise a young child on her own.

Grandma Josie and Grandpa Frank, who both taught me to be kind, humble, and respectful.

To my stepfather, Pete, and my two younger brothers, Peter and Vincent, for always supporting me through all of my entrepreneurial journeys, both good and bad.

Of course, and most importantly of all, I want to thank my wife, Bridget, for your unconditional love and support, even though my crazy ideas almost made us go bankrupt more than once.

To my children, JJ, Zach, and Brooklynn: know that everything that I do is for you three.

Braden Pollock: for allowing me to speak onstage at your conference, although I was not even invited, and for introducing me to the legal marketing world.

Seth Price: who was at Braden's event, taking copious notes, and who hired me to be his SEO consultant for his then-small law firm. I am so sorry for dragging you into the SEO game; your hair was pitch-black when we met, not so much these days though.

Harlan Schillinger: the godfather of legal marketing. Thank you for always going out of your way to make introductions, and for welcoming me into your circle; I am honored to call you a friend.

Ken Hardison: for being one of the pioneers in the legal marketing industry, while providing an educational forum for lawyers across the country to learn, network, and grow their law practices. You have had a tremendous impact on the lives of many, including me, and I will forever be grateful.

Alex and Yvette Valencia: for pulling me back into the legal industry after I sold my last agency and thought I was going to be a professional tennis player. Seriously, you guys are the best and I am grateful for our partnership.

Jacob Malherbe: for making countless introductions and endorsing me as your "SEO Guy" to some of the biggest lawyers in the country. Well guess what, you are my "Facebook Guy," and I am blessed to have you in my life both personally and professionally.

Don Worley: for being filthy rich and throwing the best parties.

Paul Faust: for being a genuinely good human being and the life of the party; thanks for so many great laughs over the years.

Michael Mogill: thank you for taking the legal marketing industry to the next level; your vision and leadership are both inspiring and invigorating. I am grateful for your friendship.

Cameron Herold: my executive coach and one of the primary reasons I wrote this book. Thank you for passing along all of your wisdom, for making tons of introductions, for holding me accountable, and for helping me grow both personally and professionally. I am truly honored to call you my coach.

Scott Shrum: my "second in command" and one of the smartest people I know—a Jeopardy champ and an M.I.T. graduate with a Kellogg MBA. Had we been in high school together, my grades would have been much better, because I would have strategically sat next to you in class. Thank you for your leadership, thank you for proofing this book and for all your suggested edits, and thanks for being a role model to the entire Hennessey Digital team.

Michele Patrick: my CFO, and what a dream it is to have you on our executive team. If it weren't for you taking so much off of my plate, with both finance, HR, and stress, as a true perfectionist, I would never have had the time to write this book. Your work ethic is admirable, and I am grateful to be on this journey together.

Lauren Holstein: my editor. Thanks for spending the past eight months of your life working with me on this manuscript. You are so awesome at what you do, and I am excited to work on my next book together.

Kathryn Lundberg: my amazing executive assistant. Thanks for not quitting when I told you that your first project was going to be reading this manuscript, line by line, and basically writing and rewriting each chapter. Thanks for making me look smarter than I really am, with your editorial guidance, and for making my life much easier by having you in my corner.

Mike Rohde: the best Sketchnote illustrator in the world, whose illustrations have been featured in one of my personal favorite New York Time's bestselling books, *Rework*. Thanks for taking on my project, and for helping me communicate my ideas, visually, for this book.

Hennessey Digital clients: without you, none of this would be possible. I know you all have so many options when it comes to your digital marketing, and I thank you for entrusting my talented team and me to design, implement, and execute your strategy, and get you more cases, each month, while growing your firms exponentially year after year.

The entire Hennessey Digital Team: to quote Steve Jobs, "It doesn't make sense to hire smart people and tell them what to do; hire smart people so they can tell us what to do." I am blessed to have such an incredibly talented team, with an amazing culture, who take complete ownership of their specific roles and functions, who teach me new things every day, while servicing our clients with white-glove treatment.

The entire SEO Industry: for all of your continued collective wisdom, knowledge, and insights. Together, we've created some of the best friendships anyone could ask for. We are a small but fierce industry of people who all stick together.

All of my friends, colleagues, and family: I love you all!

God: thank you for all your blessings, for the strength you give me, each day, and for all the people and opportunities that you bring into my life.

Thank you to the hundreds of lawyers who allowed me to reverse engineer your digital marketing strategies, without even knowing that I was doing it, over the past twenty years.

And, finally, thank YOU for investing time in reading this book. While I appreciate you taking the time to read my acknowledgments, I am disappointed that you have not started implementing some of the SEO strategies already. Remember, in life, you have the power to create a future that wasn't going to happen; all you need to do is take action. Action creates results. What are you waiting for?

CPSIA information can be obtained
at www.ICGtesting.com
Printed in the USA
LVHW090916180821
695569LV00002B/211